# Count it All Joy!

Sermonic Stories of Disappointment,

Deliverance and Restoration

## DEBRA L. HAGGINS

12/15/13

Deaconess Marian Reed,
God bless!
Debra Haggins

# Praise for *Count It All Joy!*

While you're thanking God for how He blessed, delivered and healed you, just imagine for a moment what it would have been like if God had not come to your rescue. Reminisce for just a minute what it would have been like if God did not show up on time. What it would have been like if God had not prepared a table before you in front of your enemies. Whether you are in a struggle, just coming out of a struggle or headed into a struggle, PLEASE DON'T FORGET TO THANK GOD FOR WHAT DID NOT HAPPEN!

—Excerpted from *Count It All Joy!*

*Count It all Joy!* As you read this book you get stories, real life stories and mental pictures; the visual imagery of a preacher's soul. A preacher's sermons have to come from somewhere; and these sermonic stories have come from deep within the preacher's soul. This book is by no means a normal collection of sermons. These are stories that not only preach, but help. The Reverend Debra Haggins is not only the first woman chaplain of Hampton University, but she is numbered among the greatest women in our time to serve in ministry. Read this book, *Count It All Joy!* You will be blessed.

—A. C. D. Vaughn, Past President,
Hampton University Ministers' Conference
Senior Pastor, Sharon Baptist Church
Baltimore, Maryland

Published by
One Book and a Dream Publications
debrahagginsministries@outlook.com
Phone: (757) 912-3865

ISBN: 978-0-9896223-0-1

Cover Design by Wendy Ronga/Hampton Design Group
Interior Design by Jessica Tilles/TWA Solutions.com

Unless otherwise indicated, all scripture quotations are taken
from the King James Version of the Bible.

*Written Completely…*
for the Glory of Almighty God!


*To my mother:*

The Honorable Eloise Maxine Williams

Your wounds hath healed me

that my wounds may heal others.

Thank you…

I love you…I miss you.


*For my children:*

Brian, Steven and Bradley Haggins

With all my love; all of it,

Mom

# Table of Contents

# Acknowledgements

*E*very accomplished task and each reached goal is never achieved in isolation. There are no words to express how much the love and support of a few special people have meant to me over the years. I am grateful to have this time and space to thank a few people who have consistently shared their support, love, gifts, time, talent and resources with me so unselfishly.

To God be the glory for my wonderful sons: Brian, Steven and Bradley Haggins and amazing grand babies: Isaiah, Kyle, Kayla, Jaden and Bria Haggins. I would like to praise God and thank Him for my grandparents, Mack and Mattie Williams, who have gone to be with the Lord; for my sister and nephew, Robbie Jackson and Eric Keith

Jackson, Jr., and for my cousin, Mildred Jones. Mildred, God's timing is always perfect!

To Brenda and Rory Cobb, Valerie and Wendell (posthumously) Johnson, Gloria and Dennis Walker, Rose and George Duke, thank you for your love and support over the years. You have been great friends to me.

Joanne Haggins, we have been friends since I was five and you were six. Thank you for being there for me. Thank you for sharing your family and so, so much laughter. Thank you for hours and hours of unforgettable conversations and a deep friendship and sisterhood I will cherish forever.

To Dr. William R. and Mrs. Norma B. Harvey, your confidence in me is simply amazing. I am forever grateful and awed by your support, your service to others and your great sacrifices for the cause of a better world; and Mrs. Doretha J. Spells, thank you for being a model of strength, loyalty and dedication to a cause and a mission so much greater than our individual selves.

I am indebted to my spiritual fathers and mentors for their patience and investment of time and energy in my life: Dr. Geoffrey and Rosetta Guns, Dr. Peter M. Wherry and Dr. A.C.D. and Lillian Vaughn. Also, I acknowledge the contributions of Dr. Cedric Kirkland Harris who has gone from labor to reward.

And, most importantly, thank you, Jesus!

# Foreword

$\mathcal{W}$ho has not come to realize personally and intimately that life is hard? Life is filled with sorrow, disappointments, pain and loss. Job said it like this, *Man born of a woman is of a few days and full of trouble* (Job 14:1). Jesus, the master of the art of living, affirmed, as He walked the earth, clothed in human flesh: *In this world, you will have trouble, but take heart! I have overcome the world* (John 16:33 NIV). There is no denying that in this life, we will have trouble, but through faith in Christ, we can triumph over our troubles, our trials and come out victorious.

Reverend Debra Haggins makes this crystal clear, as she opens the pages of her own life, allowing us to peep inside her private world through this collection of sermons. Her transparency is refreshing and arresting at the same time. It disarms us and invites us to take an honest look at our own circumstances and the challenging times we go through, without denying that our pain, our disappointment, grief and loss are real. It's not easy for some of us to admit that we have these difficult emotions as Christians. Some would ask, "How could we be in the faith and be sad, distressed, and discouraged?" But all emotions, even the difficult ones, are evidence of our humanity, as well as the fact that we were created in the image and likeness of God.

It may not be easy for us to admit our pain and be transparent about our pain, but it is a sign of emotional health and maturity. It is our transparency, and our honesty about our pain that is the first step to our healing and restoration, as Reverend Haggins shows us. Our transparency is also the means by which we bring healing to others. The genius of Reverend Haggins' writing and sermonic utterances is not only the affirmation that trouble doesn't last always, but that God is able to do amazing things in and through us, even in the midst of our pain and suffering. God never wastes a hurt; God takes messes and makes miracles. As you will see, her calling to preach and pastoral ministry, as well as these sermons, were birthed out of turbulent tribulation.

So, if you are going through a difficult time, I don't know of a better book to be reading. As you move through the pages, you will discover what God can do through a person who is totally sold out to Him, even when that person is in pain.

—Cynthia L. Hale, Senior Pastor
Ray of Hope Christian Church

# Prologue

# Please Read This First

*P*raise the Lord! It is an honor for me that you are considering purchasing this book. Thank you. Please know that this first literary effort is a labor of love from me to the world. I offer to you, the potential purchaser and the committed reader, a glimpse into a life (my life) filled with much that living has to offer. Except for in the case of my mother, I reveal no names, no specific situations, and no absolute or approximate locations. This is a collection of twelve, synergistic, expository-lived experiences, whereby the only thing I lay bare is my heart.

From my heart has sprung the wellspring of my deepest troubles and my greatest joys. From my heart, my preaching heart, my broken heart and more often than not my hilarious heart, I offer to you what the Lord God has deposited in me: the proclaimed word of God through my unique and often misunderstood personality. What you get from me in these pages are nuances of pain and disappointment, nuances of life's highs and lows, nuances of hard fought triumphs and serious defeats. Understand this, that even as you are reading these words, I still have not learned how to protect my heart. I need Jesus! I always have, and I always will. He looks out for me; He keeps me. He loves me.

I must say this: If you are looking for perfection in style, homiletical tradition or rhetorical execution, then you won't like this book. If you are looking for the next great American novel, put this one back immediately and I am sorry to disappoint you. If you are looking for a quick fix, an exposé on deliverance or a series of dry sermons firmly situated like a twelve-step program for the bruised, the bewildered and the broken, then this might not be what you need.

However, if you are seeking to understand through one woman's testimony that troubles don't last always, then take this book to the checkout counter immediately and demand that the cashier complete your transaction with the quickness. If you want confirmation of the fact that God is committed to your complete and total healing, keep reading; the small monetary investment you make in this book can only bring you the motivation and the inspiration you need to trust God (and for some of us the confidence to trust God, again). If you are looking to find within yourself the hope, the salvation and the joy I have always found in Jesus Christ, I welcome you. I beseech you, my brothers and sisters, by the mercies of Almighty God to allow these sermonic stories to bless you and lead you to your own personal healing and endearing relationship with our Lord. When it was dark and I couldn't see my way through, I literally preached my way out of depression, despair and a vicious cycle of abandonment. These are just a few of the preached words that literally saved my life. I didn't bleed out, because Jesus had already suffered, bled and died for me. Let my wounds heal you, that you may then be able to heal others. I believe that is the Kingdom strategy of God's one another plan.

Should you be willing to trust a novice writer with a few moments of your time, I believe that you, too, at the end of this offering will be able to...Count it all joy!

# SERMONIC STORIES: MOVEMENT I

## Disappointment

*But He was wounded for our transgressions; He was bruised for our iniquities: the chastisement of our peace was upon him; and with his stripes we are healed.* —Isaiah 53:5

*N*othing—absolutely nothing—begs a serious reality check like loss. When my mother passed away, my life changed. The earthly life force that had sustained me, encouraged me and had been there for me was no longer with me. It was the first time I seriously put pen to paper, seeking an outlet, relief and catharsis for my pain. I wrote my first play, "The Longest Goodbye," out of a personal abyss of disbelief, disappointment, loss and grief, desperately avoiding this unbelievable vacuum of what would become the new normal; my life without her.

If I could simply find my way through the unfamiliar terrain of tears and the impending reality of motherlessness, maybe I could muster the heart and the strength to bring this theatrical production to the stage. Just maybe I would find a fellow sojourner or two along this path of God-induced, God-sanctioned abandonment who would pay attention to my story. Little did I know there was another stage for which God was preparing me. According to the perfect plan of God for my life, I would write from sacred thought. God would anoint me and bid me to come to the sacred stage and speak sacred words from the sacred desk. I did not know that open wounds, emotional wounds, leave internal scars that sometimes are never meant to heal completely, but to become a source and a wellspring of healing for others. Physicians call it scar tissue.

The lowest, yet the greatest, common denominator for me in this season was having the privilege of meeting the woman at the well again, but seemingly, for the first time. At the proverbial well, God afforded me—a certain woman living in the context of modernity—the holy companionship of another certain woman—straight out of antiquity—one encounter, one sacred conversation, one glimpse into my life and then one offering of living water that only He can give. My thirsty soul, parched from loss, was quenched by an encounter; my laborious journey toward healing was induced by His presence. It was an encounter that made us both run, scar tissue intact, and evangelize our worlds even to include those who had contributed to our pain and beckon them this in our individual voices, "Come; see a man who told me all about myself." I needed that encounter—not a chance meeting— but a personal intimate encounter with the Lord. I needed healing.

# CHAPTER 1

# When You Have Been Wounded

*Who has believed our message and to whom has the arm of the Lord been revealed? He grew up before him like a tender shoot, and like a root out of dry ground. He had no beauty or majesty to attract us to him, nothing in his appearance that we should desire him. He was despised and rejected of men, a man of sorrows and familiar with suffering. Like one whom men hide their faces He was despised, and we esteemed him not. Surely He took up the infirmities and carried our sorrows, ye we considered him stricken by God, smitten by him and afflicted. But He was pierced for our transgressions, He was crushed for our iniquities; the punishment that brought us peace was upon him and by his wounds we are healed. We all like sheep have gone astray, each of us has turned to his own way; and the Lord has laid on him the iniquity of us all.* — Isaiah 53:1-6

How do you say goodbye to someone whom you have loved all of your life? Well, that day came for me when I received a phone call in the middle of a high school English lesson to come to the phone because my mother had had a heart attack. I had no details; neither did I know what to do or what to say, except to keep telling myself, "She's strong, she's a survivor, and everything is going to be all right." I prayed and I cried; I cried and I prayed. The secretary prayed with me. The principal of the school ministered to me. We sat in the cafeteria waiting for the next phone call. Finally it came. And the voice said, "Debra, she's gone." My best friend had left me. What was I going to do? Everything changed. Life had lost its meaning. Suddenly, I had become wounded. I went to get my sons, and when I saw them coming toward me, waving and smiling, I realized that what I had to tell them would be difficult, but in the blink of an eye, I became a wounded healer.

It was now that I had to make my open wounds of sadness, grief, fear and abandonment, and yes, anger, the source of healing for my sister, my children, and my grandmother. It was now that I had to bring my wounds into the service of others and in the process, not cause undue harm or injury to them. It was now that I had to minister out of the injured places, the broken places, the ripped open spaces of my life.

I came to realize at that moment that I am the product of every place I have been, every life I have touched, every life that has touched me, and everything I have ever experienced. I had to bring it all to bear and muster the strength and the bearing of a military officer for those who needed me more...they, too, were now wounded.

Therefore, I made funeral arrangements when no one else could because they all were so overcome with grief and loss. We all were severely wounded by her leaving. I, too, was grieving, but from the Spirit of the Living God came an incredible strength. The places of healing within me moved the boundaries and the parameters that would have held me back so that I could accommodate them with care and compassion, love and understanding, forgiveness and fellowship and the same sense of community that my mother had provided for me all of those years. And now that she was gone, immediately, I had to carry on the legacy of love and honor she left behind.

But in the middle of all of this, the most miraculous thing happened: My mother's death gave birth to my preaching ministry. Through hurt, confusion, woundedness, and in the middle of my pain, I communicated the Gospel of Jesus Christ from the sacred desk for the first time in the form of her eulogy. A ministry was born; God had called me to be His preacher and told me that there was a pastoral call on my life. My call to preach was birthed out of my brokenness. With shaking hands and a trembling voice, a preacher was born and my life has never been and shall never be the same again.

The Prophet Isaiah teaches us and prophesies to us in this familiar passage of scripture the coming of the ultimate wounded healer. He calls Him, "Suffering Servant." We call Him Jesus Christ, Immanuel, Mary's baby, Lamb of God, Holy One, Savior, Redeemer, and Son of the Living God. In three divisions, Isaiah dissects the life of the One who had not yet come. In verses 1-3, Isaiah describes the Servant's lowly existence. He has:

- No special form
- No special beauty
- Nothing in His appearance to make us desire Him
- Nothing in His form to make us take notice of Him
- He was hated of men
- Rejected by people
- Yet, He took upon Him our suffering
- Yet, He became acquainted with grief.

In verses 4 and 5, Isaiah describes the agonizing death of the Servant stricken, smitten and afflicted by God. Isaiah goes on to report that we saw His suffering and thought that God was punishing Him. But Jesus was wounded for the wrong we did. HE took upon Him our suffering and felt our pain. HE was bruised and crushed for our evil. Isaiah also identifies the honorable purpose of the Servant; that our purpose was to heal mankind by way of His stripes and His wounds that would take away all of our sin and iniquity. In other words, the punishment that made us well, the punishment that made us whole was given to Jesus. Why? God did it because we are just like sheep that are prone to go astray and need a Shepherd. Why? God did it because we are just like sheep that are prone to wonder and desperately need a Savior.

As I look at life from a very human perspective, I have observed that we want to, relish in doing things our way without honoring or even considering God's way. Like sheep, we can be easily misguided and obstinate. I read somewhere that of all of God's animals, the sheep is the least able to take care of itself. Sheep need a guide. Sheep are defenseless. Sheep have no fangs, no claws, and cannot bite. In other words, just like sheep, and even as we are professing Christians, we cannot make it through life by ourselves. We, too, are defenseless and have no protection against the evil that abounds in the world without the protection of a Mighty Shepherd. We are blessed because we serve a wonderful Father who loves, cares about, feeds and tends His sheep and His lambs. However, at times, we fail to rely on the guidance of the Great Shepherd only to find ourselves lost and out of the fold of protection. Many times, it is only after we have been wounded, and in turn have wounded others, that we look to Jesus Christ to rescue us from our pain. I am so glad these experiences have taught me that Jesus will not rest until, will not stop searching until that one sheep that became lost or strayed from the pathway of safety is back in the comfort and security of the fold. He is the Great Shepherd!

This chapter goes on to describe in graphic words the physical, mental, and emotional wounding of our Lord and Savior, Jesus Christ: Even though He was beat down and punished, oppressed and afflicted, He never said a mumbling word. He, in turn, became like a lamb, being brought to the slaughter, but He was quiet like a sheep while His wool was being cut from His body. Jesus was cut off from the land of the living, even though He had done no violence and had no deceit in His mouth. But verse 10 reminds us: *of the divine truth that because God loved us so much, it pleased Him to bruise His Son, and to make the soul of His Son an offering for the sins of the world.*

There we have it: the length, the width, and the depth of a man's life; the fact that we live, the fact that we die and the fact of our purpose for living (for existing) lies somewhere in between. Over the course of a man or a woman's existence, we will be scarred by the situations and the circumstances of life. Being wounded is on the spiritual itinerary of every Christian. Our spiritual resume must include suffering. Our wounds draw us closer to Christ. We all vicariously, and through our very own life experience, become suffering servants and wounded healers.

And, yet, the relevant question that emerges is: What do we do with the wounded? What does the Church do with those who have been scarred before they enter these doors? What do we do with the wounded who come to church Sunday after Sunday, listening for some word from God? What do we do with the wounded who come, listening for a word that will ease the pain and the stresses of life? How does the community of faith respond to those whom Jesus calls "the least of these"? How should the faith community respond when a brother or a sister feels that no one cares? What does the faith community do for the disenfranchised? For those of us to whom life has been kind and the troubles have been few, what are our responsibilities to the homeless, the defenseless, and the broken? Where is the Balm in Gilead that is meant to heal every sin-sick soul?

God wants us, the community of faith, to respond to the wounded among us with a passion for the restoration of personal faith, a passion for the breaking forth of unborn hope, and with a passion for instilling of agape love that will make the salvific power of Jesus Christ a reachable, touchable apprehensible reality.

God wants us to respond to the wounded among us, with our own personal testimony of restored faith, renewed hope and of how the agape love of God made the salvific power of Jesus Christ a reachable, touchable apprehensible reality in our life. How do we begin to take on this awesome ministry of compassion and restoration? God wants us to contemplate for the purposes of greater understanding a few things about coming to the aid of the wounded and the walking dead among us.

God wants us to know that just because a person is not bleeding does not mean that his/her wounds are any less severe.

Around us every day are people who have been wounded by arrows of loss and heartache that they carry on the inside."

We were meant to notice another's pain. *We* were meant to notice, not just their smile, but their pain; not just their title, but also their pain; not just their bank accounts, but also their pain! Notice somebody's pain other than your own and offer help.

Too often we admonish others to "keep a stiff upper lip" when those same lips are parched from thirst or chapped from the cold, or trembling from crying.

We hear people tell us that we should be grateful that "things aren't any worse than they are." That's easy to say when you haven't been diagnosed with terminal cancer, or when you're facing eviction, no lights, no heat, no gas, water cut off, or telephone disconnection.

Sometimes we tell people that "time heals all wounds." In all actuality, time doesn't heal anything! Only God can heal! There are times when time just magnifies the pain! We get comfortable and we forget to remember these words: "If it were not for the grace of God, I just might have had to walk a mile or two in your shoes." It's hard to hear those words when an individual has to live a life that's hard and go through pain that is real.

But we are mandated by Christ to look for those who are wounded and hurting among us. Look for those church members among us who have been injured by the slings and arrows of outrageous fortune. Look for the wounded. Look for the injured. Look for the walking dead among us.

Why? Because in one way or another, we have all been hurt. In one way or another, we all are hurting. Every single one of us is in the same boat.

- The laughing, the smiling, the happy-go-lucky, the nonchalant

- The apathetic, the aloof, the proud, the introvert, the extrovert

- The anti-social, the asocial, the maladjusted, the well adjusted
- The shouting saint, the reserved saint
- The clown, the comedian, the life of the party
- The solid, the surefooted
- The dependable, the irresponsible
- The unemployed, over qualified, the under qualified
- The unloved, the unlovely, the beautiful, the homely
- The rich, the poor — we are all wounded in one way or another
- Those of us whose dreams have collapsed into oblivion
- The confused, the left out, the disenfranchised
- The hungry, the homeless, the hopeless, the hapless
- The misunderstood, misrepresented, under-represented, not represented
- The disrespected, disavowed, disenchanted, the despondent, the disconsolate, the alcoholic, the drug addict

Every person on Earth carries the burden of pain and hurt. But Isaiah lets us know that we don't have to carry these burdens alone. The text states: *Surely He took up all our infirmities and carried ALL of our sorrows, ye we considered him stricken by God, smitten by him and afflicted. But He was pierced for our transgressions, He was crushed for our iniquities; the punishment that brought us peace was laid upon him and by his wounds we are healed.* In the midst of pain and hurt, we have a burden-bearer.

God wants us to realize that we may never be healed until we realize how badly we have been wounded.

Through the generation of new cells, the body provides coverings (natural coverings) that begin to form over open wounds. These scabs, no matter how badly we have been scarred, remain in place until a new layer of skin covers the wound underneath.

If we remove the wound's natural scab too early or before it is time, the wound reopens and feels as painful as it did when the old wound was new. God wants us to be honest with Him and honest with ourselves about just how badly we have been wounded. As much as friends and family want to help, only God empowers us to dig deeply enough to heal our deepest pain.

Stepping into the role as a wounded healer makes us recognize and examine the irritants that could remove our natural healing agents. Those natural healing agents are faith, hope, love, joy, peace, longsuffering, patience, kindness, forgiveness, compassion, and commitment. I am committed to my healing and the healing of others.

I wonder if I could have recognized my own wounds as still being open, but covered with the bandages of self-reliance and self-denial. I wonder if I merely bandage the wounds repeatedly, only to find out that when the artificial covering was lifted, these wounds were still open and still sensitive to the irritants of light and heat. What emotional antiseptics did I use? What emotional antiseptics do we all use? Do we merely mask the pain to give ourselves temporary relief to wounds that go deep beneath the surface of the epidermis of our daily lives?

A little more than ten years after the sudden and unexpected death of my mother from a massive heart attack, I am still saying goodbye. At times, I am still nursing the wound that refuses to heal. I chose to reflect upon this period in my life as a wounded healer after walking the corridors of Norfolk General Hospital one Friday on a visitation assignment. I chose to reflect upon this period of my life because I believe that there have been times when I have not facilitated my own healing process very well. To properly care for this wound, would be to force me to release my mother, to let her go and to deny her continual entry into my daily life. I don't know if these wounds were meant to heal, or if they were meant to be a source of healing for others. I have come to realize that it is through the saltiness of my own tears, the saltiness of my own life that others will be healed and find true liberation in living the Christian life.

One of the great life deposits from this experience is that God wants us to know that He allowed woundedness to come upon us so that our wounds might heal others.

John and Paula Sanford, in their book, *Healing the Wounded Spirit,* talk about something called "see-through faith." This is the kind of faith that looks beyond our present circumstances and our current situations so that we might celebrate what the Lord is accomplishing by way of the very struggles we are involved in and maybe even frustrated by at this present time. I biblically characterize see-through faith as the substance of things hoped for, and this substance of what I we cannot see right now. I don't see my healing, but I know it's on the way! I don't feel a breakthrough, but I know that it's on the way! I don't see deliverance anywhere in sight, but I know it is right around the corner.

- Why? Because faith in God allows me to "see-through" the mess and see my Jesus!
- Why? Because faith in His promises according to His Word allows me to "see-through" the eyes of my Savior and know these afflictions will last only for a little while.

- Why? Because I can "see-through" the eyes of my faith, grace and mercy declaring that I am no longer a victim.
- Why? Because I can "see-through" the eyes of faith and know that I can use my wounds as a source of healing for others who cannot "see-through" the darkness for themselves.
- Why? Because while we are yet in the labor of our own pain, we can labor, no we must labor with others until we see the light of Christ shining forth in them!

It's similar to what John says in John 16:21, *Whenever a woman is in travail, she has sorrow, she has pain, but when she gives birth to the child, she remembers her anguish no more, because even in pain, new life has been birthed into the world.* There comes a time in the life of every wounded soldier when in order to survive and not be captured by the devil's trap, he has to push through some stuff!

- PUSH…through the pain!
- PUSH…through the sorrow!
- PUSH…through the hurt!
- PUSH…through the ridicule!
- PUSH…through what your mama did!

- PUSH …through what your daddy did!
- PUSH…through your disappointments!
- PUSH…through heartache!
- PUSH…through heartbreak!
- PUSH…through the unemployment lines!
- PUSH…through the glass ceiling…break it if you have to!
- PUSH…through the disrespect and dishonor of every misogynous bigot who told you that you couldn't preach God's gospel and He didn't call you to stand in His pulpit!

When I say push, all I'm doing is taking the letters of the word push, placing them in an acrostic context and saying…PRAY UNTIL SOMETHING HAPPENS! If you want your healing, PUSH! If you want your deliverance, PUSH! Pray until something happens!

What do we do with the wounded? Teach them to declare that they are no longer a victim and…

PUSH! PRAY UNTIL SOMETHING HAPPENS!

Over many years, in listening to the war stories and testimonies of brothers and sisters in Christ, I discovered, somewhere along the line while attending to the needs of others, that I was still dealing with my own pain, disappointments, and shortcomings, and have emerged each time calling myself unworthy of the confidence my God has placed in me. I have been moved and touched by the strength and the depth of the conviction of fellow saints in the midst of horrible situations.

But most of all, what I realized and discovered is that we have all answered the call of God through cracked vessels. Life has wounded us all. People have dropped us. Our families may not have understood us. The world does everything it can to discredit us. And yet, there are those of us who are still giving it all up, going for broke, selling out, putting it all on the line and laying it all down for the sake of the call of God upon our lives.

And I have concluded, for those of us who were wounded, that it was by the grace of Almighty God that brought us through the valley of the shadow of death. Only God who could have brought us through:

- Some dry places
- Some hard places
- Some rough places
- Some tough places
- Some dark places
- Some terrible places

- Some tight spaces
- Some embarrassing places
- Some disgusting places
- Some brokeplaces
- Some downright ugly places
- Some ungodly places
- Some unholy places
- Some places of disillusionment
- Some places of abandonment
- Some places of disappointment
- Yet, Lord, even after I had made it through and had come to realize that my healing was not complete, my prayer is simply, Lord:
- I know I don't deserve it, but I'm asking You for my healing!
- I know I don't deserve it, but I'm asking You to bless me!
- I know I don't deserve it, but I'm asking You for a home in Your Kingdom!

Jesus found one more chance to live out His role as a wounded healer, and even on the cross, He said to one dying thief, *Verily, verily I say unto thee, you shall be with me in paradise.* Jesus used this opportunity to give hope to a dying, wounded thief.

We have that same hope. It's a hope that says, GOD EVEN IF YOU DON'T CHANGE THE SITUATION, JUST GIVE ME PEACE IN THE SITUATION!

The scripture says, *Now abide faith, hope and love! And the greatest of these is love!* There is still good news for the hurting and wounded. There is still good news for those of us who are going through, have been through, or on the way through!

It's good news for the wounded to know that we serve a God who loves us! If you've ever been wounded, betrayed, violated, had a door slammed in your face, bitten by a snake, stabbed right down the middle of your back and left to die, hurt and abandoned on the side of the road, then have faith in God. Have hope in the resurrection power of an all-wise Savior and know that the love of God and the power of the Holy Spirit will heal your wounds because there is a Great Physician! When you have been wounded, walk by faith; persist in hope and then just rest in the bosom of God's love!

# CHAPTER 2

# A Serious Reality Check

*Before I was afflicted I went astray: but now have I kept thy word. Thou art good, and doest good; teach me thy statutes. The proud have forged a lie against me: but I will keep thy precepts with my whole heart. Their heart is as fat as grease; but I delight in thy law. It is good for me that I have been afflicted; that I might learn thy statutes. The law of thy mouth is better unto me than thousands of gold and silver.*
—Psalm 119:67-72

*N*othing means more to me than my relationship with God, and so it should be for those who love the Lord, and are called according to His purpose. For those who love the Lord, I sincerely hope and pray there is nothing that means more to you than your relationship with God. For those who love the Lord, there is embedded in that relationship a dependence and a love for the Word of God that is unexplainable, yet inseparable from whom we are as children of the Most High God. I cannot explain it; I simply accept it by faith! I accept the fact that all of my help comes from the Lord! I accept the fact that apart from God, I am nothing and can do nothing! I accept the fact that He saved me, because He loves me. I accept the fact that He delivers me because He loves me. I accept the fact that He justified me because He would not have me to perish! I accept the fact that God is the source and the strength of my life! I accept the fact that a life without the Word of God is simply no life at all.

There is life in the Word! The Word has a sobering effect. Everything else pales in comparison to the Word. Relief is in the Word! Release is in the Word! Salvation is in the Word! Whatever I need is in the Word. Do you want to know who Jesus is? You will find Him and find out about Him in the Word! In the Word, I find my help, my encouragement, my outlook, my direction, my instruction. I would not want to go about the business of living without the Word. It is my guidebook, my rulebook. I've learned to take corrective action according to the Word. You know corrective action: *the battle is not yours; it belongs to the Lord!*

You know corrective action: *having done all to stand, keep standing!* You know corrective action: *Sit while I make your enemies a footstool for your feet!* You know corrective action: *Fret not yourself over evil doors for in the end they shall be cut off.*

There is a blessed assurance in obeying the Word. Cleansing comes by the Word. Discernment comes by the Word. I get my sense of insufficiency through the Word. There is power in the Word. We can persevere because of how God strengthens us with His Word. I get victory through the Word! My breakthrough comes by way of the Word. Rest and comfort come through the Word. The Word holds me through good times and holds me in bad times. It holds me amidst good report and amidst evil report. We gain greater insight through the Word! I am sustained by the Word. My prayer, my praise and my proclamation are rooted and grounded in the Word! When I need a serious check on life, I retreat to the Word, particularly Psalms. People usually turn to Psalms for encouragement, strength, and hope.

Psalm 119 takes the form of a personal testimony, but the main purpose of this psalm is to glorify God. Even the cries and the laments of the psalmist has at the core of its purpose that even in sorrow, every earnest heart should give glory and honor to God. In each verse, as the psalmist checks in with his reality, his perception of his own predicament and his reflection and contemplation of his own life, he also has a fit of praise. His check on reality brings his praise. It is as though he stops and says, "I can remember when I did not have it together, when I was a wretch undone, but at the mention of your name, at the remembrance of all the good you have done for me and to me, I can't help but give you glory, I can't help but give you honor and I can't help but give you praise."

Psalm 119 is not an ode to joy, but an ode to the Joy Giver. The psalmist does this by remembering, by looking at his own life and at the benefits of living life according to the Word. Then he takes a serious reality check on what it means to live apart from the Word of God and contrary to the very nature of God. His reality check brings him to the understanding that there is a very high standard to which God is calling all of us. There is a narrow path; a narrow way and exact prescription we must fill if we are going to live life in Christ. The psalmist realized that even though he cannot stop life from happening, he could control the way he reacts to it, so he contemplates and then concludes that: the Law of God is perfect because it converts the soul. The Testimony of God is a sure thing because it makes the simple wise. The statues of God are right; it makes the heart rejoice. The Commandments of the Lord are pure, as they give light to the eyes. The fear of the Lord is eternal, and endures forever. The judgments of the Lord are true;

His judgments are altogether righteous. This writer came to the serious realization that you cannot take a piece of the Word of God and obey the part that makes you comfortable. You believe either all of it or none of it.

It seems kind of elementary, kind of immature to take the letters of the alphabet and write such a powerful praise. But, sometimes, when life becomes difficult and chaotic, and reality becomes distorted, that's the time to break the problem down to its lowest common denominator, down to its basic elements, down to the core of the matter and simply tell God how you feel. I still believe that if I tell God all about my problems, He will work it out for me. I still believe God is a way maker! I still believe He is a burden-bearer! I still believe He is a heavy load sharer! I still believe He can and will save! Therefore, at the base of the situation at hand, the psalmist realized that no matter what he had seen, no matter what the opinion of others may be, or may have been, he came to know and understand a few very real conclusions: God's law is a gift! God's law teaches us! God's decrees are precious! God's statues endure! And, finally, that God's Word speaks to us!

Under the inspiration of the Spirit of God, the psalmist takes the mechanical monotony of a simple literary tool called an acrostic poem, and uses all twenty-two letters of the Hebrew alphabet to pour out his whole heart and tell the world what the Lord means to him. How did he do it? He took twenty-two letters, approximately two thousand six hundred words, one hundred seventy-six verses and then divided those verses into twenty-two sections and gives each section eight verses. Each one of those twenty-two sections is identified by the alphabetical order of the Hebrew lettering system. Has your heart ever been so full of praise for God that you just don't know what to do? You try and tell Him thank you, but it's not enough.

Maybe the psalmist was saying, "I will take everything that I have at my communicative disposal and try to explain to everybody or anybody or somebody what the Lord has done for me, how the Lord has delivered me, what the Lord has stopped me from worrying about, what the Lord has done for me."

In the first section of the psalm, he was testifying about the blessings of obedience. In the second section of the psalm, he was testifying that the cleaning of a life comes only by the Word of God. In the third section, he was letting us know that sometimes walking with God is difficult! Walking with God is not easy, but rather than become bitter and angry, he thanks God for the privilege and the experience.

In the fourth section, he testifies that there is strength in understanding that when trouble comes, call on God for strength and reach into the Word of God for understanding. Call on God and if He doesn't reveal it to you right now, you will understand it better 'by and by.' In the fifth section, he testifies that we all need guidance. In the sixth section, he asks God to give him the courage to witness to kings without being ashamed and to call on God to be His source of his comfort.

In the seventh section, the psalmist resolves that it has not been by any works of his own hand or by anything that he has done, but the faithfulness of God's Word in his heart has kept him. He writes in the 57th verse, *I have said that I would keep your words, that I would think upon your words, that I would meditate upon your Word. And now I can turn my feet only to your holy testimonies and give thanks to my God.* It is at this point that the psalmist has a serious reality check and in verse 67, he gets real sober and remembers this: *Before I was afflicted, I went astray, but now I keep your word.* He literally looks back over his life, and he thinks things over and literally has a ten-word testimony:

## "IT IS GOOD FOR ME THAT I HAVE BEEN AFFLICTED."

The reality check is whereas he went astray before he was afflicted, he now sees the benefit of that same affliction. I see it, too. I didn't see it then, but I see it now. Let me explain. It was the affliction, it was the turmoil, it was the hard times, it was the trouble, it was the hardship, it was the depression, it was the difficulty, it was the mess, it was the rejection, it was the sleepless nights, it was the weary days, and it was the betrayal that made me understand if I never had problems, I would have never known that God could solve them. There is a benefit and a purpose in our suffering.

Everybody reading this sermon has had some kind of a testimony. This is where the testimony of the psalmist and the testimony of the modern day saint intersect.

Before I was afflicted, before I had trouble, before I was trying to work it out in my own strength, I went astray. The psalmist said it this way, *Before I was afflicted, I went astray."*

Here is the great transformation! Here is the great deliverance! BUT NOW, I keep Your Word. But I will keep Your precepts with my whole heart. But I delight in Your law. But now — after a serious reality check — I keep Your Word. But now — after an extreme makeover — I keep Your Word! But now, I realize that You are good! The psalmist wrote, *God You are good and You do good!*

You might say it like this: I like the way You bless me; God teach me Your statutes. I like the way You protect me; God teach me Your precepts. I like the way You comfort me; God teach me Your commandments. I like the way You watch over me; God teach me Your ways. I like the way You answer me; God, teach me Your testimonies. I like the way You light my path; God teach me Your Word.

In other words, when I learned some stuff and experienced some stuff, when I came to myself, when I look back over my life, when I did a serious reality check, I realized (look at verse 72) that *The law of Your mouth is better to me than thousands of coins of gold and silver.* I thank you for the gold and the silver, but Your Word is better to me than…I thank You for the…But Your Word is better to me than…I thank You for the…But Your Word is better to me than…

Unlike the psalmist, I don't know Hebrew. However, like the psalmist, I, too, can use the twenty-six letters of the English alphabet for a serious reality check:

- A—He anointed me.
- B—He blessed me.
- C—He went to Calvary for me.
- D—He died for me! He delivered me!
- E—He empowered me!
- F—He's been a Father to me!
- G—He gave me grace!
- H—He healed me!
- I—He invited me to come on in where the table is spread…
- J—He justified me!

- K—He kept me!

- L—He liberated me!

- M—He moved me!

- N—He never left me alone!

- O—He opened doors for me! He offered me the gift of eternal life!

- P—He promised me! He purified me! He has been patient with me! He preserved me!

- Q—He quickened me!

- R—He rescued me!

- S—He sanctified me!

- T—He touched me!

- U—He underwrote me a lifetime warranty!

- V—He gave me victory! And if that was not enough…

- W—He went up Golgotha's hill for me and went all the way to hell and back for me!

- X—He removed the X factor for me! You see, it's not an unknown, I know my Redeemer lives!

- Y—He yielded my temptations!

- Z—He raised me to my zenith.

If you have had a reality check and you now believe that it was good for you that you were afflicted, you ought to praise Him!

# CHAPTER 3

# A Spiritual House Cleaning

*And God, which knoweth the hearts, bare them witness, giving them the Holy Ghost, even as He did unto us; And put no difference between us and them, purifying their hearts by faith. Now therefore why tempt ye God, to put a yoke upon the neck of the disciples, which neither our fathers nor we were able to bear? But we believe that through the grace of the LORD Jesus Christ we shall be saved, even as they. Then all the multitude kept silence, and gave audience to Barnabas and Paul, declaring what miracles and wonders God had wrought among the Gentiles by them. And after they had held their peace, James answered, saying, Men and brethren, hearken unto me. — Acts 15: 8-13*

$\mathscr{N}$o matter how long you have been preaching, you still never really feel ready when the preaching moment comes. There are still feelings of inadequacy and fear. No matter how long or how well you preach, there are still those feelings that make you wonder if the audience will like you or not. Each Sunday, we place a request before God that the word will change somebody's life and turn around his or her situation. We pray that the prepared word, the preached word, and the spoken word will give someone new life and new hope.

The Bible calls it "the foolishness of preaching." It is what one has called the "bittersweet moments of the prophetic pastime called the sermon" that we are charged and must maintain the integrity of the pulpit at all costs. As we examine the spiritual inventory of a pulpit ministry, we realize there are certain things expected of the preacher. It is expected that there must be a certain level of self-composure. You don't get too loose and forget where you are standing. Preacher, this is holy ground! It is expected that there will be a certain eloquence of speech. You must communicate the word clearly and succinctly.

We should be able to follow your choice of text throughout the message as you avoid jumping from scripture to scripture without a clear path to the resolution of the conflict between the thesis and the antithesis and without an answer to the relevant question. Just stay focused. You can't tell it all in one message. There is a non-negotiable expectation that there shall be a certain level of order maintained in the pulpit and a certain level of decency upheld by the 'pulpiteer' when approaching the sacred rostrum. Don't turn backflips and spin off the back of chairs, and don't do cartwheels. Preacher, don't turn God's pulpit into a three-ringed circus. We did not ask for a stand-up comic, nor a ringmaster or a toastmaster.

However, all we ask you to do is stand flat-footed and just preach the gospel like your life, and every life under the sound of your voice, depends upon it. PREACHING IS A MATTER OF LIFE AND DEATH! I agree, wholeheartedly, that the preacher should have a certain physical presence, mental stability, moral acuity and an exuding spirituality that is efficacious, infectious, and addictive. There should come from the preacher a holy impartation that forces one to preach the three-fold scandal of the crib, the cross, and the crown to bring forth its undeniable relevance in our lives.

Yet, when it is preaching time, it is hard to keep your composure when you have had a trying week and you have talked to others who have had a rough week and even a rough life. It is hard to remain eloquent. It's hard to be stale, dry and quite proper when all you want to do is holler and say, "God is good all the time; and all the time, God is good!" It's hard to do that when all you want to do is holler and say, "I said I wasn't gonna tell nobody, but I just couldn't keep it to myself." It is hard to maintain order in the pulpit when sometimes the preacher feels like running, shouting, dancing, and clapping.

It's hard to maintain order in the pulpit when the 'pulpiteer' hears somebody shout, "Glory!" over there, "Hallelujah!" on the other side, "Jesus!" in the back, "Thank you, Father!" on the left and "Praise Him!" on the right. It is hard to maintain an elegant posture when somebody yells "Preach!" and you know that there is only one person holding the mike! It's hard to remain calm when you hear the choir sing, "You are the source of my strength. You are the strength of my life. I lift my hands in total praise to you!" It is about that time that all you want to do is turn around and tell those folk who are looking at you funny, "Baby...you have no idea...that I WILL become even more undignified than this!"

Caesar Clark, pastor of the Good Street Baptist Church in Dallas, Texas, says, "All of your life, preaching will tease you and taunt you. And when you come to the end of the preaching moment, when you come to the end of the prophetic opportunity, you will have to say that your preaching has been nothing more than an embarrassed stammering before God's people." That is to say that after the sermon, we sometimes think about what we could have said and what you should have said. Then, after everybody has gone home, we find ourselves back in the study, praying for forgiveness and then asking God for a second chance to get it right the next Sunday.

In "The Gospel According to Luke," we find that the first three chapters deal with the birth, boyhood, baptism, and background of Jesus. Chapter 4 roughly through 9 emphasizes His temptation in the wilderness, the calling of the twelve and His earthly ministry. Jesus announces His ministry and pronounces the authority of His ministry over demons, disease, his disciples, over defilement by healing a leper, and over defectiveness by healing a man with palsy. He preaches the Sermon on the Mount and outlines the activities of His ministry whereby He ministered in sickness, in death, in the midst of doubt, and, most of all, He ministered to sinners.

When Jesus invited the disciples to go over to the other side and ministered in storms, he asked the disciples, "Where is your faith?" Jesus ministered over demons by asking a wild man, "What is your name?" Jesus ministered to a woman who was in despair and touched the border of his garment by asking, "Who touched me?" He ministered to His disciples and to the physical needs of the multitudes. Jesus was rejected by men, yet was received at Bethany. But throughout the ministry and the rejection He experienced, Jesus kept on teaching on the Kingdom of God and the repentance and salvation of humankind. He taught concerning hypocrisy. He taught concerning covetousness. He taught against blasphemy. He taught concerning faithfulness, and repentance. Jesus taught a lot about people: inflexible people, inflated people, invited people, uninvited people, indifferent people, and indulgent people. Jesus tells us all to count up the costs of full commitment to Christ in a life of service. However, this brings us to Chapter 15, how Jesus taught concerning God's unfailing love for sinners. And He does this using the parable.

In the beginning of this message, we took a spiritual inventory of the preacher and the pulpit to uncover and refine the art of preaching with integrity. It is in this same light, this light of recovery, this light of finding lost things that the Spirit of the Living God presses each of us to take an inventory of our lives and quite possibly do a spiritual house cleaning. In this text, we find the little parable, a story of a lost coin. It is stuck right between the parable of the lost sheep and the lost son. Jesus is teaching and still trying to get these Pharisees to understand that His ministry was a ministry to seek and to save the lost.

And so he narrates a short story about a woman who has ten coins and loses one. It is written that Jesus asks, *Isn't it reasonable to think that this woman will light a lamp and scour the house looking in every nook and cranny until she finds the one coin that is lost?* I like the way the King James Version records it: *What woman, having ten pieces of silver, if she loses one piece does not light a candle, sweep the house, and seek diligently until she finds it?* And when she finds it, you can be sure that she will call together her friends and neighbors and say, "Rejoice with me for that which is lost is now found! Be happy for me; for I have found the piece, which I had lost!" Jesus goes on to say that in this same way there will be that kind of a celebration, there will be that kind of rejoicing in the presence of God's angels every time just one sinner repents.

Therefore, what can be more appropriate than taking up the issue of housecleaning, spiritual housecleaning that is. Many times in life, we come to the place whereby in the midst of the clutter and the daily routine of living that some things we value and treasure and some things we need to carry on life, according to the plan of God, get lost. We hear about spring-cleaning — setting aside a time for cleaning the house from top to bottom. However, we will come to realize that in the life of the Christian, taking a spiritual inventory of our lives can happen at any time of the year, and any time of the day. Taking a spiritual inventory of our life and our church is always in order. Every Christian has to check his/her connection at some point in time. In fact, for us to keep our lives in line with the Word of God, we must not fail to do some heavy duty clearing and cleaning of our individual lives, some heavy duty clearing and cleaning of our spiritual lives as individuals and as a body of believers who come together to worship and to praise our God. That is to say that in this spiritual housecleaning, we might find that our God is seeking to organize or re-organize all things so that we might find those precious treasures that are somewhere in the house, but somehow got lost in the house.

Spiritual housecleaning involves getting our affairs in order before God takes a holy audit of our lives, and so before God comes to "shake the house," I need to do some spiritual housecleaning. Before Jesus comes and shines the light in the house, I need to do a spiritual housecleaning. Before Jesus comes and sweeps the house, I need to check every corner, check every nook, check every cranny where the devil may have tried to enter my life and infiltrate my thinking, steal my joy, kill my dreams and destroy my destiny. I need to do some spiritual housecleaning. God wants us to take inventory of our lives and clear out the clutter so that we might find those lost things in our lives. What is God's plan for finding lost things? What is God's plan for a spiritual housecleaning?

### Light a Candle

The first thing this woman did when she was looking for the lost coin was to shed more light on the situation. She lit a candle and started looking for what was lost. With increased visibility, she was able to see into some dark places that she would not have been able to look into had she not increased the light and decreased the darkness. Some people don't like the light because it makes an already bad situation seem worse. But just as the Word says, *how can they hear without a preacher*, I ask, "How shall we see without the light?" What is that light? It is the light of God's Word, which cuts deeper than any two-edged sword. The light reminds us all that Jesus came so that we might have life and light and have them both more abundantly.

We are reminded that we must walk in the light. When we have lost our peace, when we have lost our joy, when we have lost contentment, it is imperative that we look to the Light of God: *My Word is a lamp unto thy feet and a light unto thy pathway.*

### Sweep the House

Not only did the woman shed more light on the situation, but she also swept the house to find what she had lost.

And so we do as the woman did who lost the coin, we sweep the house until we find what we have been looking for. We sweep the house until we find that thing which was lost. Sweeping the house has a double blessing, because as we are looking for what we lost, we also find some stuff that we should have thrown out a long time ago. We find some stuff that other folk left behind. When we do this spiritual housecleaning when we find some things that we lost, we will find some things that we don't need in our lives: foul spirits, unclean spirits, cantankerous spirits, uncooperative spirits, and lying spirits. Sweep the house! Take out the trash!

But if it's still valuable and useful to you, keep it! Keep love! Keep joy! Keep peace! Keep happiness! Keep your sweet disposition! Keep good friends! Keep your family! Keep a positive attitude! Keep a holy outlook! But most of all, if the item serves no good purpose, if the item serves no good use, if the item is just taking up space, if the item is an eye sore, if the item is causing clutter, if you keep tripping over it and stumbling over it and its causing you more trouble than it is worth, get rid of it!

### *Just Keep Looking Until You Find It*

I've lost some things and I want them back! I've misplaced some things and I want them back. Some stuff slipped through my hands and rolled out of my sight! And so I'll count up my coins and I'll come to the reality that something is missing! With all that you have done for me, there is still a void in my life! With everything that I have accomplished and everything that I have accumulated, there is still something missing. So I'll keep looking until I find it!

It's time to do a spiritual housecleaning! We have got to wake up one morning and set in our minds that this is the day that the Lord has made and we will rejoice and be glad in it. Glad that I've got another chance to sweep the house. I'll need to erase some dumb stuff from my memory bank. I need to flush out my drain, get rid of all the negative thinking and flush out all the junk that other folk have left behind. I need to organize my life, straighten out my thinking, check my water purification system and change my water purifier to make sure that I drink only from the Living Water of Christ so that I will never be thirsty again. I need to dust out the cobwebs of the past. Change my furnace of affliction to a soul that is on fire for God. Remove the ashes from the fireplaces and replace it with the beauty and the joy of the Lord. Clean all of my downspouts and roof gutters that block my blessings. Replace every faulty part that hinders my praise. Remove all of the junk that clogs up my worship. Replace and fix all of the broken equipment in my life that won't let me get a prayer through to God Organize loose keys and throw away old keys to doors that God locked a long time ago that I keep trying to open. Remove every insect and every pest that comes to bring a pestilence to destroy the destiny God has for my life. Clean out my storage bin of old grudges and old memories.

Finally, when I take out all of the trash, all of the junk and all of the garbage put on the side of the curb, I'll say, "God I thank You for your Holy Light! Thank You for another opportunity to sweep the house!" When I turn around and go back into my house, a spiritually-clean house, a house that has been organized and set in order by the Master Planner Himself, one who specializes in finding lost souls and finding lost things and restoring lost people, renovating run down lives, revitalizing areas of mental, physical and emotional blight, then and only then will I be able to go back to a spiritual house cleaning where God is already at work, giving this temple a spiritual makeover. God refuses to make it over before he cleans it up!

God will paint the walls of my life with the love of Christ! God will polish my life with the joy of the Lord. I'll wash all of my windows and screens so that my vision will be clear because I'll have Jesus on my mind and heaven in my view. Then I'll be able to say, "God make my heart your home."

# CHAPTER 4

## "If"

*Then saith Pilate unto him, Speakest thou not unto me? knowest thou not that I have power to crucify thee, and have power to release thee? Jesus answered, Thou couldest have no power at all against me, except it were given thee from above: therefore he that delivered me unto thee hath the greater sin. And from thenceforth Pilate sought to release him: but the Jews cried out, saying, If thou let this man go, thou art not Caesar's friend: whosoever maketh himself a king speaketh against Caesar. When Pilate therefore heard that saying, he brought Jesus forth, and sat down in the judgment seat in a place that is called the Pavement, but in the Hebrew, Gabbatha. And it was the preparation of the passover, and about the sixth hour: and he saith unto the Jews, Behold your King! But they cried out, Away with him, away with him, crucify him. Pilate saith unto them, Shall I crucify*

*your King? The chief priests answered, We have no king but Caesar.* —John 19:10-15

We take so much for granted—the food on our tables, the clothes on our backs, and the roof over our heads. Abraham Maslow theorized that we all have certain basic needs that must be met. These basic needs, which are the key to life, are many times the things we most often take for granted. If you have never been hungry, you would not understand someone else's need for nourishment. If you've never been homeless, you won't understand what it means to be without shelter. If you've never been cold or have never failed, you won't understand what it means to be warm or to succeed. If you have never fallen, then you don't know what it means to be saved. If you have never been sick, then you don't know what it means to be healed. If you have never been poor, then you might not understand the value of a dollar. If you have never been disenfranchised, left out, abandoned, cast out, set aside, crushed, or perplexed, then you wouldn't know what it means to be accepted and included unconditionally.

From his work, *As You Like It*, William Shakespeare said, "All the world's a stage, and all the men and women merely players; they have their exits and their entrances, and one man in his time plays many parts, his acts being seven ages." However, I still believe that we can attest to the fact that God is a mighty good God, and it is great to be alive. It is great to be alive because we serve a God who has forgiven us of our sins. The Apostle Paul said that *where sin abounds, grace abounds much more.* But are we so foolish as to take God's forgiveness for granted and just keep on sinning?

So often in my prayers, you will hear me tell God, "Not only do I love you," but also "God I appreciate you." In other words, I am trying to say, "God, Your value does not depreciate with time. Your worth does not diminish in time, but God I appreciate You because You did not have to bless me. You did not have to save me. You did not have to forgive me. You did not have to consider me and pick me up. You did not have to look beyond my faults and see my needs. God, I appreciate You because You have been faithful and just, merciful and kind, loving and forgiving, gracious and patient. And for every blessing extended to me in the name of grace and mercy, I just want You to know that I do appreciate You! You see, the older I get the more I realize that I'm alive because of God's faithfulness.

"Lord, I just don't want You to think that I have become full of myself and have forgotten where all of my help comes from. I don't want You to think that I could have come this far in my own strength. But I appreciate how You watch over me, both day and night. God, I love You, but that's easy for me to do. You don't ask much. I don't just want to say thank you; it just isn't enough for all that You've done for me.

"But when I consider and reconsider your goodness in my life and what could have happened, all I have to do is take a little word, the little two-letter word "if" and preach it within the context of a grateful heart. All I have to do is take this little word "if" and reposition it out of the position of supposition, possibility and assumption. All I have to do is take this little word "if" and reframe it from a negative context, give it what psychologists call a positive reframe and make some great, life-affirming affirmations that go something like this: If you call on Jesus, He will answer your prayers. If it had not been for the Lord on my side, I would have been consumed. If I go into my secret closet, the Bible tells me and my personal experience tells me that He will meet me there. If I never had problems, I would never know that God could solve them. If God is for me, who can be against me? King David in Psalm 139: *Where shall I go from your spirit or where shall I flee from your presence? If I ascend up into heaven, you are there: if I make my bed in hell, behold, you are there. If I take the wings of the morning, and dwell in the uttermost parts of the sea; even there shall your hand lead me, and your right hand shall hold me. If I* say, *surely the darkness shall cover me; even the night shall be light about me*. In the heat of disappointment, my success, my healing, my deliverance depends and hinges on the strength of the "if factor" in my life.

I also see the "if factor" in the story of Jesus. Listen to Him tell his own story:

*Pilate had made attempts to release me and proposed to my haters and would be accusers and executors that I be scourged, beaten and then let go. There was a custom at the time of the Passover when the Jews had the privilege of having a prisoner released to them at the discretion of the governor. At the time of my trial, there was a prisoner named Barabbas, a violent man, who was being held on charges of murder and sedition. Pilate wanted to save me and thought that the religious leaders would surely release me and carry out the sentencing on Barabbus. However, it became clear to Pilate that these who gathered, these who spat on me, these who would pluck the hairs from my beard, these who came to abuse, and torture me were determined to kill me. Pilate declared, "I will give this man a good beating and then I will let him go." Yet in the middle of the accusations, it was the peace of God that engulfed me and allowed me to hold my peace; I never said a mumbling word.*

*It was at that moment, as the shouts of the crowd grew louder, a messenger came and handed Pilate a note. It was a message from Pilate's wife who advised her husband to have nothing to do with this ordeal, for I was an innocent man. Pilate's wife told* her husband that she had been tossing and turning all night because of the fact that she had a terrible dream; a nightmare.

From what I could see, Pilate now was more determined than ever to set me free and there was one more possibility. There was one more thing that he could do that surely would release him from the pain of indecision. And then he turned his attention to the crowd and told them, "I am about to set one man free: he is a murderer; he is an insurrectionist against the Roman government. I can set him free or I can release to you your king. What do you want? Who will it be?"

And the response from my killers was "Give us Barabbas!" They all responded in one voice, "Give us Barabbus! We don't want Jesus, give us Barabbas!" Pilate was shocked! His final attempt to release Jesus had failed. Pilate thought, "Maybe if I bring him out and place Jesus who claims to be the Son of God and Barabbas whose name means "son of the father" surely they will come to themselves and realize that this man has done them no harm. Maybe if I place the killer next to the Savior! Maybe if I place the man of war next to the Prince of Peace. Maybe if they see this hardened criminal on my left and look over and see a harmless peasant they will change their minds. How can they receive Barabbas and reject Jesus? How can they allow jealously to cloud their judgment?" But all of Pilate's logic, all of his reasoning, every attempt he made to save me fell on deaf, cold and blood thirsty ears.

*I knew now; I was very aware that I had been rejected on three fronts: first the chosen people of God had rejected me, then the heathen had rejected me, and now it was Satan himself who showed up in the form of a criminal name Barabbas. Barabbas didn't have to do a thing but just stand there and the enemies of God who had now fully embraced the mission of Satan would do all of the work for him. Pilate pleaded with the mob again, "Look at these men. I bring them both before you. You see life, and you see death. You see a future and then you see no hope. Who will it be? Will it be Barabbus, or will it be Jesus also called the Messiah?" And once again, the chief priests and the Elders shouted "Give us Barabbas! You can keep Jesus, just give us Barabbas."*

*"I have told you that this man is innocent! Herod has told you that he finds no fault in this man. Why are you allowing envy and jealousy to cloud your judgment?" And they shouted once again, "Give us Barabbas!" In other words, it was as if the religious leaders and my despisers were shouting, "Give us death; give us hell; give us the grave!" The religious leaders were declaring that any man claiming to be the Son of God cannot live!*

*Pilate then called me back inside of the palace walls and asked me, "Who are you?" And I still said nothing! Frustration, confusion, perspiration, filled every crack and crevice of my face. And then he said, "Don't you know that I have the authority to set you free or to put you to death?" And it was at this moment* that I looked Pilate in his face and said, "You are a government official, a puppet of the Roman government, you have no authority over me. The only reason you have this authority is because it was given to you by my Father which is in heaven."

In determined frustration, Pilate tried once again to release me, but the Jewish leaders all shouted, "Not this man, but give us Barabbas! If you release this man, you are no friend of Caesar." And Pilate's question to the unreasonable ones was, "What then shall I do with Jesus?" Their response, "Crucify him! Give us Barabbas, but crucify Jesus!" What do you mean! Crucify your King? Behold, your King!" But they shouted louder, "Away with Him; away with Him! Give us Barabbas!" Pilate said to them, "Shall I crucify your King?" The chief priests answered, "We have no king but Caesar."

But Pilate, looking out for his own best interests knew that if a riot broke out on Roman soil, then the governor would be sent back to Rome in shame. Pilate now, in every failed attempt to set me free, called for a basin of water and said to the Sanhedrin, "I find no fault in Jesus. I am innocent of this man's blood. If you want him dead, then you crucify him!" And then with even more venom and hatred, they shouted to the applause of Satan and all of hell, "Then let his blood be on our heads."

And so then the Roman guards took me to a little room; shoved me inside, stripped me of the purple robe that Herod had give me, took branches and thorns and wove a crown that they smashed into my skull. The crown of thorns tore my skin *and ripped my forehead. The blood came streaming down. They gave me a wooden stick and called it a scepter. They laughed at me and mocked me and called me the King of the Jews. They grabbed the same stick and beat me with it. They beat me until the stick punctured my flesh and blood flowed. I was even more unrecognizable. Then they took me where the other condemned prisoners were awaiting execution. Barabbus had been released, and I Jesus was condemned to die. And the rest of the account of my passion, I believe you know all so well.*

*It was at this moment in the Passion narrative that I received a new revelation from God that made me realize that Pilate may have let Jesus go had if it not been for a statement from the Chief Priest that began with the little word: IF YOU RELEASE THIS MAN, YOU ARE NO FRIEND OF CAESAR!*

What do we do with the "if" situations in our lives? What do we do in times of instability and uncertainty?

First, God wants you to know that just because you wash your hands does not mean that they are clean. Pilate thought that by washing his hands he would not be held responsible for the death of Jesus. However, he was just as responsible for the death of Jesus as Judas, as Caiaphas, as the seventy Elders of the Jewish Priesthood, as Pilate, as Herod, and as the violent mob, the Roman soldiers who whipped him, as the onlookers who spat on him and everybody who picked at him. They were all guilty.

Pilate thought that by a symbolically washing of his hands he could erase the guilt and the stain of handing over an innocent man to the bloodthirsty cries of an angry mob. But if we would look at this situation more closely, we will see that Pilate should have washed his hands before he turned an innocent man over to die. I was standing over my kitchen sink and washing my hands when the revelation hit me. You don't wash your hands after you eat. You wash your hands before you eat. The Holy Spirit revealed to me that Pilate should have washed himself clean of injustice. He should have washed himself clean of a self-serving attitude. He should have washed himself clean of revenge. He should have washed himself clean before he allowed the Sanhedrin to get him dirty and completely contaminate his life with the guilt and the sin and stain of crucifying the Son of the Living God. I believe that God would have anointed him and give him the power to say no to Caiaphas and his mob. Pilate was a leader, who washed his hands, but washed them too late. Saying "I'm sorry" wouldn't fix it. Saying, "I didn't mean to do it" or "I didn't know" wouldn't fix it! Washing his hands was just a symbol. It was a symbol that showed that Pilate was a coward who wanted to do the right thing but couldn't.

In this life, when it comes to right and wrong, you've got to do more than just wash your hands. In fact, if you are going to wash your hands, wash your hands before the fact and not after the fact.

Finally, God wants you to realize that He is the only one who can turn your "if moments" into "but God" moments. We have all been like Pilate at some point in life; juxtaposed between right and wrong. Pilate was wavering between saving his own skin and setting free the Son of God. Bad things happen when we waver. Bad things happen to good people when we bargain with the devil. Bad things happen when we esteem anybody or anything over the power, the will and the favor of God! When we wallow too long in our "if moments," when we are juxtaposed between suppositions, let me tell you what happens: The devil has a chance to come in and sow seeds of doubt. The devil has a chance to make a case against Christ. The devil has a chance to make you doubt the Word of the Lord. The devil has a chance to question the power of God to change your life. It is my understanding, according to the wisdom of the Bible, that a double-minded man is dangerous in all of his ways. The devil has a chance to make me a double-dealing, two-faced, double-hearted, suspicious, distrustful, paranoid schizophrenic who will yield to a crowd that would dare say, "Give us Barabbus!" We see Jesus, but give us Barabbas.

And we find ourselves, just like Pilate, juxtaposed between our faith and our failure. We find ourselves somewhere between what the people might say, what the people might think and what is right in the eyes of God.

We have all had "if moments" juxtaposed between the faith of God and the lure of the world, between salvation and sin, between righteousness and riotous living and between what I what I should do and what I want to do. Then somehow, we come to ourselves, step out of a place of juxtaposition and move into a position of: "just suppose" I trust God with my whole life!

Just suppose I stepped out of indecision, indetermination, obstinacy, uncertainty, hesitation, fluctuation, vacillation and wavering into the center of God's will that "if factor" will turn into some serious "but God" moments: but for the grace of God it could have been me; but for the mercy of the Lord; but for the compassion of God; but for the Holy Ghost power...

Pilate never came to himself. He thought he was innocent, but he was just as guilty as the Sanhedrin. So now, the ball is in your court. The decision is yours. Who will it be? Will it be Barabbas or Jesus?

# SERMONIC STORIES: MOVEMENT II

## Deliverance

*Sing, O barren woman who did not conceive; for the children of the barren woman shall be more than the children of the married wife.* — Isaiah 54:1

*I* love this verse from Isaiah 54. It is more than wonderful, more than amazing how one passage of scripture can reveal such a powerful metaphor for one's life. It seemed a bit strange to me that I would whole-heartedly embrace such a passage in light of the fact that

I have given birth to three sons. Yet, for so many years, I considered myself to be counted among the most barren of women and no one knew. However, the barrenness I felt was not due to a fruitless womb, quite the contrary. However, the barrenness I felt and needed deliverance from was the product of an unfulfilled life. I dreamed dreams; I preached sermons, I had visions of being used greatly and mightily by God; yet I could not conceive that there would one day be so great a harvest. While I loved God with all of my heart, He directed that I should spend some time in the wilderness where I could meet Him again and allow Him to re-introduce Himself to me as Lord of the Harvest.

Barrenness, in the metaphorical sense, is a matter of not producing results in our families, churches, finances, health, friendships and, even as importantly, within ourselves. Barrenness is the reaping of an unwanted harvest because of sowing or broadcasting seeds of apathy to avoid disappointment, seeds of rejection to avoid getting hurt, seeds of pride to avert vulnerability, and seeds of perfectionism to avoid the pathology of internal and external criticism. Barrenness evolves over years and years of unresolved issues, unanswered prayers, unaddressed situations, unmanageable circumstances, unbelievable disloyalty and dire straits. Through the process of working, and at times waiting on my personal deliverance, I prayed this one scripture from Psalm 91:4: *Lord, I believe that you will cover me with your feathers, and under your wings I will find refuge; your faithfulness will be my shield and my rampart.* Before my state of consciousness would stabilize, before my quality of life would change, before deliverance would come for me, I had to learn to move with what God divinely provided for me in this season. I had to know that God had gone ahead of me and provided the cloud by day to guide me and the pillar of fire by night to give me light. Deliverance came for me by His guidance and His light, His shade and His shield. God did just what I asked Him to do. He covered me.

I have to give God praise for Jesus; while I waited on God, I gained powerful revelations, mighty blessings, redemptive end products and life-affirming takeaways from my time in the wilderness. I learned how to love people who did not love me in return. I learned how to bless and not curse when the latter and not the former seemed more appealing. I learned that it was my duty to love folk anyway. I learned—not after I got out of the wilderness—while I was still in that barren place, while I was still on bended knees to thank my God for what didn't happen. I thank God for deliverance.

# CHAPTER 5

# In the Meantime

*Then the word of the LORD came unto me, saying, Before I formed thee in the belly I knew thee; and before thou camest forth out of the womb I sanctified thee, and I ordained thee a prophet unto the nations. Then said I, Ah, Lord GOD! behold, I cannot speak: for I am a child. But the LORD said unto me, Say not, I am a child: for thou shalt go to all that I shall send thee, and whatsoever I command thee thou shalt speak. Be not afraid of their faces: for I am with thee to deliver thee, saith the LORD. Then the LORD put forth his hand, and touched my mouth. And the LORD said unto me, Behold, I have put my words in thy mouth. See, I have this day set thee over the nations and over the kingdoms, to root out, and to pull down, and to destroy, and to throw down, to build, and to plant. Moreover the word of the LORD came unto me, saying, Jeremiah, what seest thou? And I said, I see a rod of an*

*almond tree. Then said the* LORD *unto me, Thou hast well seen: for I will hasten my word to perform it.* —Jeremiah 1: 4-12

$\mathscr{A}$ccording to William Barclay, even when a man or woman discovers the task for which God has sent him or her into the world, he or she still has another problem to solve. It is the problem of when to begin that task for which he or she has been so aptly and so duly called. If one begins too soon, he/she will suffer the consequences of being ill prepared and will begin without the necessary preparation and equipment for the task. If one waits too late, the individual may never begin the task at all. If the individual begins at the wrong moment, then his or her work will become victim of wrong timing and may be doomed for failure even before the process begins. Timing is everything[1].

Dorothy Norwood sings, "He is an on-time God; and that He may not come when we want Him, but that He is always right on time." From the Book of Ecclesiastes, King Solomon, the philosopher, the proclaimed wisest man who ever lived, was perplexed about life and concerned about the way he had spent his life. However, while he was seeking to discover the meaning of life and trying to figure out why, after having accomplished so much, he was still unfulfilled, and dissatisfied with his life and utterly disillusioned about the whole duty of man, Solomon came to the conclusion that life is quite simply about time and that there is a right time for everything. He believed that in every man's life and in every woman's life, depending upon the atmospheric conditions of the situation and the environmental climate of the circumstances there comes an opportune time to move. King Solomon writes that there is:

- A time to be born and another time to die.
- A time to kill and another time to heal.
- A time to tear down and another time to build.
- A time to weep and another time to laugh.
- A time to scatter stones and another time to gather them.
- A time to embrace and another time to abstain from embracing.
- A time to search and another time to count your losses and give up.
- A time to hold on to something and another time to let it go.
- A time to rip out and another time to put it all back together.
- A time to be silent and another time to speak up.

- A time to love and another time to hate.
- A time to wage war and another time to make peace[2].

One great hymnologist of the church wrote these lyrics: *Time is filled with swift transition. Nothing in a stand still position, nothing in a seemingly stationary position, every situation that seems impossible, and every thing that seems immovable, nothing on this earth unmoved can stand! There has to be a shift in the paradigm, change and transformation is inevitable THIS IS WHY, we must build our hopes on things eternal and hold to God's unchanging hands.*[3]

I have come to listen to the spirit of the text and understand how the Bible implores us to explore and embrace living life as a wheel within a wheel. It is (God's time) or kairos time which is symbolized by the big wheel, and the measurement of man's time or chronos time, which is symbolized by a little wheel. This little wheel is the vehicle by which we measure our days, hours, minutes and seconds of lives. It doesn't matter how many times we as a society spring forward or fall back in the name of daylight's savings time. When we leave this earth, we all must spend eternity somewhere. Whether we count the minutes like sand through the hourglass and determine, declare and decree, like MacDonald Carey, that these are the days of our lives, we all must spend eternity somewhere.

Whatever is our mission or God's mandate upon our life, whatever it is that God has called us to do, no matter how long it takes for God's ageless purposes for our lives to come to pass, we must know and understand that the plan for our lives was set in eternity before the foundation of the world.

Every now and then, we have to be reminded that life is too short, death is too sure, hell is too hot and eternity is too long for us to spend precious time lying, gossiping, backbiting, scheming and conniving, dealing in subtle or covert sabotage or bold in-your-face sabotage. And there is not a devil from hell, in hell or around hell that can rip God's perfect plan for our lives out of His hands.

Use the power of visual imagery to catch this principle of Kingdom living. Our purpose is positioned in the little wheel of life and then situated in the middle of the big wheel of Eternity. It is the little wheel that turns swiftly and one day shall cease, but even after the little wheel of life stops turning, we quickly and swiftly move into the center of the big wheel. However, the eternal big wheel does not turn but goes in a forward motion. Time, and how you use it, is the responsibility of man! Eternity *is* the responsibility of God.

However, in order to move into the Eternal Wheel, we must now redeem the time because *only* what we do for Christ will last. It is *our* responsibility to make sure that we make the most of these days; it is each man and woman's individual responsibility to make sure that we use time for the purposes of the good of the Kingdom (God's Eternal Kingdom).

Therefore, it behooves us not to wait until life is almost over, or until we are on the bed of affliction, or until we are deep in trouble to say, "I had better get busy for the Lord!" Or "Lord, if you just help me out this mess I won't do it again! I'll serve you! I'll live for you! I'll be a witness for you!"

We must begin investing now, working now, living now, serving now, and giving Him praise now in *all* things and in *everything* because these are the things that are going to make a difference in our lives when we step out of time and into eternity.

The quality of our lives on earth must resemble the life we hope to live when we die. In other words, we must not wait to begin Kingdom living when we get to the Kingdom; we've got to start living it right now, before it is too late. We dare not wait until we get to heaven to start acting like we are citizens of heaven. We must start living now like we've got Jesus on our minds and heaven in our view.

Whether it is Central Time, Pacific, Standard Time, Mountain Time or Greenwich Meantime, we had better remember it is as the saints of old used to say, "Time, time, time, time is winding up! Don't you see how this world has made a change? Preachers tell your members that time is winding up! Fathers, tell your sons time is winding up. Mothers, tell your daughters time is winding up. Don't you see how this world has made a change?"

There is a window of time and a window of opportunity. Something we call THE MEANTIME that makes the difference in the way we live our lives, and where we will spend eternity. And what makes the difference between our success and our failure is what we do with something called THE MEANTIME. It's that in-between time. It's that time of life when we are betwixt and between the promise and the fulfillment of something God promised us a long time ago.

So whether in the meantime we waste time, or hoard time, or borrow time, or buy time, hate time, make overtime, time-and-a-half or double time, or whether we lose time, misuse time or abuse time, count time, mark time, laugh in the face of time, or even if we come to a clear understanding that an untimely death is the enemy of time, know one thing that is certain and sure: THAT ONE DAY, ALL OF US WILL RUN OUT OF TIME!

However, I'm so glad that through the trials of life, there is One who holds my hand. That's good to know because I don't know about tomorrow. I just live from day to day. There are many thoughts about tomorrow I don't seem to understand, but my confidence lies in the fact that I may not know who holds tomorrow. However, I do know who holds my hand.

Our text speaks about time. Along with Isaiah, Ezekiel, and Daniel, Jeremiah should be classified as one of the captivity prophets. Jeremiah literally preached and warned the people of God and their leaders about the coming of the Babylonian captivity as a chastisement for their sins. Even though the people were rebellious, hardheaded and stiff-necked, Jeremiah still preached. When their captivity was taking place, Jeremiah still preached. He preached during the reign of Josiah before the captivity. He preached during the reign of Jehoahaz. When Jehoiakim had to surrender Jerusalem to Babylon, Jeremiah still preached. When King Nebuchadnezzar, the puppet master, appointed Jehoiakim and made him a puppet king, Jeremiah kept on preaching. He preached during the puppet-rulership of Zedekiah for eleven years. Even when Zedekiah rebelled against Babylon and razed it to the ground, Jeremiah was still preaching. Jeremiah preached through all of the dark and horrible days of Jerusalem and remained in the land. Jeremiah the prophet, the preacher, did not leave the desolation of Babylon even after it was rendered a ghost town. Jeremiah preached in Jerusalem, while Ezekiel preached in the labor camps. Jeremiah preached in Babylon, while Daniel was strategically placed in the palace of Nebuchadnezzar. While Jeremiah preached, Ezekiel and Daniel were greatly influenced by his ministry. If you've ever heard or read the preachments of Daniel or Ezekiel, you've heard a little bit of Jeremiah. Not only was Jeremiah a great preacher, he was bold, he had courage, and he wasn't a coward. He didn't throw rocks and hide his hands. He went in the midst of trouble and literally preached the place out of confusion.

In the meantime, in the midst of all of that preaching, the ministry of Jeremiah is extremely noteworthy because before God called him, He prepared him. He was a man who devoured God's Word and loved it. He was told, just like Isaiah, that he might as well stop preaching because the people were not going to listen to him. Jeremiah was called to stand alone for the cause of the Word of God, knowing that he would be ostracized, despised, opposed and rejected by men. Jeremiah, Isaiah, Moses, Elijah, Jonah and Job were all prophets who, at one time or another, in their ministries wished they were dead because the burdens placed upon them by God were so heavy.

The burden of the ministry God had given to them was so great that these great prophets wished they had never been born or called. It was so hard to preach the pure Word of God because the people did not want to hear it. Much like the saints of today, everybody wants a message that makes him or her feel good. Everybody wants formula preaching. The people wanted a cute introduction with not too much background information; three points that are not too long; a traditional Black Baptist hoop, shout me a little bit, send me home, and everybody is happy! But sometimes the Word of God isn't so pretty! Sometimes the Word of God makes a saint say, "Ouch." And if you can't say ouch, just say Amen. But the preachments of Jeremiah were strong. Sometimes they were downright harsh. Who can forget the sermon of the Rod and the Almond Tree that invites us to go down to the Potter's House? Or, the sermon of the Earthen Vessel he smashed on the floor of the temple? Or, the sermon of the Two Baskets of Figs— one basket was good and the other basket was bad. Or, the sermon that described the spiritual state of the people of Judah as being rebellious, idolatrous, and sinful? Or, the sermon directed to corrupt leadership, and sermons on healing and salvation?

To what in the modern day world can we equate the ministry of Jeremiah? Jeremiah had what we call prophetic passion. How can I help you understand the passion of a prophet? When a man chains himself to a nuclear power plant because he feels the use of nuclear energy poses a threat to the world, that's prophetic passion. When someone sits at the entrance of an abortion clinic and is then drug away in handcuffs, that's prophetic passion. When a kamikaze pilot straps a bomb to his chest, runs an airplane into a building, and kills himself and everybody else, that's prophetic passion. During the Civil Rights Movement of the '60s, Black folks held boycotts, marches, and sit-ins and thus had to fight off police attack dogs, high pressure water hoses, tear gas, Billy clubs, bullets, Klu Klux Klan attacks, cross burnings, Jim Crow Laws, Molotov cocktails, and de facto and de jure segregation laws just so they could have fair and equal treatment under the law, unlimited career opportunities, fair housing status and a quality education. This is prophetic passion. Martin Luther King, Jr. had prophetic passion. Mahatma Gandhi had prophetic passion. Mother Theresa had prophetic passion. Corrie Ten Boom had prophetic passion. Elijah Muhammad had prophetic passion. Gardner C. Taylor had prophetic passion. Medgar Evers had prophetic passion. Paul and Silas had prophetic passion. Shadrach, Meshach and Abednego had prophetic passion. Matthew, Mark, Luke, John, Simon, Peter and all of the disciples had prophetic passion. And last, but certainly not least, Jesus

Christ had so much passion that surely He carried all of our sorrows and bore all of our grief, and the chastisement of our peace was upon Him.

But how was Jeremiah prepared for this mission? Where did he get his passion for God's people? How could he stand in the middle of Babylon and preach as if he had lost his mind without fear of retribution? How could he preach without the fear of what people would do to him? They couldn't shake his confidence. They couldn't scare him, intimidate him, run him off, or dig up enough dirt on him. Where did the prophetic passion come from?

In the meantime, while Jeremiah wasn't looking, God was working on him. The text informs us that God came to Jeremiah and said to him, *Before I formed you and shaped you in your mother's womb, I knew all about you. Before you saw the light of day, I had holy plans for you. I set you apart to be a prophet to the nations.* And the Holy Canon records that by Jeremiah's own admission he said, *Hold on a minute Master. There are Kings all around me with big names and big titles and high positions. There is Josiah, son of Ammon who is the King of Judah; there is Jehoiakim who is the son of Josiah, who is the King of Judah; and there is Zedekiah who is also the son of Josiah. Look at me! I am nothing! I have nothing! And if you ask some of the people, they'll tell you that I didn't come from nothing. I don't have a kingdom, Lord God; all I have to offer you is me.*

God tells Jeremiah, *Don't tell me who you are. Don't tell me what you can't do! Just do what I tell you, and you will be all right.* God said, *Jeremiah, I'll tell you where to go and all I want you to do is just go! But in the meantime, I'll put my words in your mouth, and whatever I command you to say, just say it! But in the meantime, do not be afraid of their faces. Do not be afraid! In the meantime, fear thou not, for I am with thee. Be not dismayed for I am your God. I will strengthen thee. Yes and I will help thee. And I will uphold you with the right hand of my righteousness. I've given you a job to do. I have appointed you AND anointed you to these people. Your job, Jeremiah is to pull up and tear down. Your job, Jeremiah is to destroy and to overthrow. And then, it is your job Jeremiah to start over, to build and to plant. But in the meantime, don't pull punches and don't take the stance of a coward. In the meantime, stand at attention while I prepare you for work. But in the meantime, I'm going to make you an impenetrable castle and a fortified city. In the meantime, I'll make you as immovable and as steadfast as a steel pipe, as solid as a concrete block. Jeremiah, I'll make you a one-man wrecking machine against the wiles of the devil!*

What does God want us to learn from Jeremiah's meantime experience? God wants us to know that there are two reasons why none of the civil and spiritual leaders could prevail against Jeremiah. God wants us to know that these same reasons, these same promises are available to us today. Jeremiah could stand flat-footed and powerfully and boldly preach God's message because he was assured of two things: (1) I AM with you and (2) I WILL deliver you.

First, as you are going through your meantime experience, keep your ear to the mouth of God, and He will tell you out of His own mouth, "I AM with you." That is the first blessed assurance that Jeremiah had. God said, "I am with you." This is not the first time that God told a prophet that He was with him. Moses said, *When they ask me who sent me, what shall I say?"* God told Moses, *Just tell them that I AM.* I am with you! Just as I was with Moses, Jeremiah, I AM with you. Just as I was with Abraham, I'm with you, too. I was with Noah and Job, Isaac and Jacob, David and Samuel, Hannah and Deborah, Esther and Ruth, Amos, Malachi, Habakkuk, Isaiah, Ezekiel, Daniel, and yes, Jeremiah, I am with you.

The worst thing that we know about Jeremiah is that he cried a lot. He cried so much that they called him the "weeping prophet." He cried so much that the very next book of the Bible was called the Lamentations of Jeremiah. In the midst of our tears, in the midst of our sorrows, in the midst of our fears, in the meantime, while we are waiting for the promise to come to pass, just know that God is with us. He has promised in His Word that He will never leave us or forsake us. Don't worry about what you don't have, just know that I am with you. Don't worry about what you can't do. Just know that I am with you. Don't worry about what people say. Just know that I am with you.

Aren't you glad that God is with you? In all of your trials and tribulations, God is with you. Broke, but God is with me! Tired, but God is with me! Persecuted, but God is with me! Cast down, but God is with me! Lied on, but God is with me!

And then finally, God said to Jeremiah and He's still saying to you and to me, *I will deliver you.* Jeremiah was free to move around because God assured him that even if he fell into divers hands and into dire straits, even if he got into trouble, even if he got in over his head, even if he had to fight severe jealousy, even if he had to dodge the darts of a demon who used him for target practice, God said to him, *I will deliver you.*

Jeremiah, even if I sent you into a pit of snakes, don't worry about it, I will deliver you. The same God who was in the Garden of Eden, the same God who witnessed the fall of man, the same God who saw Adam and Eve eat of the tree of knowledge of good and evil and then try to hide behind a few fig leaves is the same God who blessed them and then turned around and cursed them. He is the same God who made a serpent crawl on his belly like a snake. And so Jeremiah, if you just happen to walk into, be thrown into, get sent into, stumble into a snake pit don't worry about it Jeremiah, I will deliver you.

Because in your proverbial snake pit like the one you'll find in Babylon, you'll find all breeds and all kinds of snakes. You'll find dumb snakes, stupid snakes, mean snakes, low down snakes, dirty snakes, back stabbing snakes, crooked snakes and hard-hearted snakes. In your snake pit, you just might find greedy snakes, jealous snakes, deceitful snakes, confused and ignorant snakes, young snakes, old snakes, slick snakes, scheming snakes, conniving snakes. But don't worry about the snake pit, Jeremiah. Just know that if I sent you in, I'll bring you out. And even if they bite you, I'll make the very poison from their mouth like medicine in your veins.

But in the meantime, Jeremiah, just know that while they may have you surrounded, don't forget that I've got you covered! You're blessed and highly favored of the Lord. Know that in the meantime, my goodness and my mercy will follow you everywhere you go.

It's the same mercy and goodness New Testament believers can find in Jesus. So I am so glad that while Jesus was waiting for the call, He got to know me, in the meantime. I'm so glad that while He was waiting to save my soul, He got to know me, in the meantime. I'm so glad that while I was still a wretch, He pleaded my case, in the meantime. I'm so glad He kept me, in the meantime. I'm so glad He saved me, in the meantime. I'm so glad He loved away all my doubts, in the meantime. I'm so glad He raised me, in the meantime, so that my meantime would become God's time.

NOTES
1. William Barclay, *The Mind of Christ*.
2. Ecclesiastes 3:1-11.
3. Inspired by *Hold to His Hands*.

# CHAPTER 6

# Your Deliverance is on the Way!

*And when he went forth to land, there met him out of the city a certain man, which had devils long time, and wore no clothes, neither abode in any house, but in the tombs. When he saw Jesus, he cried out, and fell down before him, and with a loud voice said, What have I to do with thee, Jesus, thou Son of God most high? I beseech thee, torment me not. (For he had commanded the unclean spirit to come out of the man. For oftentimes it had caught him: and he was kept bound with chains and in fetters; and he brake the bands, and was driven of the devil into the wilderness.) And Jesus asked him, saying, What is thy name? And he said, Legion: because many devils were entered into him. And they besought him that he would not command them to go out into the deep. And there was there an herd of many swine feeding on the mountain: and they besought him that he would suffer them to enter into them. And he suffered them. Then went*

*the devils out of the man, and entered into the swine: and the herd ran violently down a steep place into the lake, and were choked. When they that fed them saw what was done, they fled, and went and told it in the city and in the country. Then they went out to see what was done; and came to Jesus, and found the man, out of whom the devils were departed, sitting at the feet of Jesus, clothed, and in his right mind: and they were afraid. They also which saw it told them by what means he that was possessed of the devils was healed. Then the whole multitude of the country of the Gadarenes round about besought him to depart from them; for they were taken with great fear: and he went up into the ship, and returned back again. Now the man out of whom the devils were departed besought him that he might be with him: but Jesus sent him away, saying, Return to thine own house, and shew how great things God hath done unto thee. And he went his way, and published throughout the whole city how great things Jesus had done unto him.* —Luke 8:27-39

$\mathcal{I}$t is amazing how the world chooses to reject the counsel of the Lord who can deliver us and loosen us from our strongholds. Yet, in our everyday speech, much of the wisdom we expound is heavily laden and super-saturated with phrases that come from the Word of God.

It is amazing how some people say phrases, use words, pass along wisdom that comes from God's Holy Word and never, ever give Him credit or honor for being the Author and the Finisher of their faith. It is as if we ignore the undeniable fact that all wisdom, all knowledge, all understanding begins and ends in God and with God. Have you ever heard:

- "My cup runneth over." Taken from Psalm 23:5
- "Fight the good fight." Taken from 1 Timothy 6.12
- "Many are called, but few are chosen." Taken from Matthew 22:14
- "Apple of my eye." Taken from Deuteronomy 2:10/ Zechariah 2:8
- "This too shall pass." Taken from Matthew 24:6-8
- "The truth shall make you free." Taken from John 8:32
- "There's nothing new under the sun." Taken from Ecclesiastics 1:9
- "For everything there is a season." Taken from Ecclesiastics 3:1
- "In the twinkling of an eye." Taken from 1 Corinthian 15:52

- "Faith will move mountains." Taken from Matthew 21:21

- "Signs of the times." Taken from Matthew 16:3

- "It is better to give than to receive." Taken from Acts 20:35

- "My brother's keeper." Taken from Genesis 4:9

- "The writing on the wall." Gen 4:9 Daniel 5:5

These are what the world calls common phrases that actually come directly from the Word of God. What kind of a world would accept the wisdom of God without receiving the God who is wisdom? Our God is a literal God. He says what He means and He means what He says. The Bible is the world's most beautiful work of literary craftsmanship. It is a compilation of the literary, the historical, and the theological. The Bible, that ageless, living, breathing instrument of forgiveness, salvation and deliverance is the greatest book ever written! The Bible is not an end unto itself, but a means to an eternal life of growing to know God, maintaining a personal relationship with Him and being in His perfect will. It is the immutable, unchangeable Word of God. The Word of God does a complete work in us because it delivers us from our sorry situations.

We realize that His Word not only appeals to our intellect and our spirit, but it also appeals to our senses. For as much as we are spiritual people, we are also sensory people. God loves us so much that He even appeals to our senses: see, hear, taste, touch and smell. My Bible informs me that I can *look to the hills from whence cometh my help.* That is a visible God. *O, taste and see that the Lord is good!* That is a savory God! This poor man cried out to the Lord and he was delivered from all of his afflictions. He is an auditory God and He hears me when I call. The Word assures me that *the effectual fervent prayer of the righteous profits much.* He is an available God! The scriptures remind me that *there is a time and a season for everything under heaven.* That is a kinesthetic God (He moves in His own good time and in His own good pleasure!). His commands direct me to pick up my bed and simply walk. That's a touchy-feely God.

His parables lead me to understand that if I could just touch the hem of His garment I know that I will be made whole. That is a tactile-kinesthetic God. What is it that we hear many of the saints say? "I would not serve a God that I could not feel."

I can touch the heart of my God and feel that He is at work in my situation all at the same time. I can touch His heart with my worship. I can touch His heart with a hallelujah! I can touch his heart with the pain of my infirmities! He's just one prayer away, one whisper away.

What is it that we hear many of the saints say? "I would not serve a God that I could not feel."

The Psalmist writes: *Let everything that has breath praise the Lord*. That one phrase is a call to take up spiritual arms. Don't panic, it's in the Word. When I praise God in the sanctuary, He can see it! When I praise God in the heavens of His power (not my power, but His power) He can feel it! When I praise Him for His mighty acts and His wonderful deeds on my behalf, He can see it! When I praise God according to the abundance of His excellent greatness, He can hear it! When we praise Him with the trumpet, He loves it! When we praise Him with the flute and harp, He loves it! When we praise Him with the tambourine, when we praise Him with loud, clashing cymbals and with the beat of the drum, God can feel it!

When we praise Him in the dance, by ourselves, with a partner, in a group, at our seat, down the aisle in the parking lot, on the side of the road, God sees our praise and inhabit, lives, dwells, occupies, takes up residence, finds a home and feels at home in the praises of His people! So, *Let everything that has breath praise the Lord!* is not figurative language, but a direct command.

In Luke Chapter 8, we read one of the most well-known stories of deliverance. It's a miraculous healing and emotional healing by Jesus of a demon-possessed man who was possessed by a "legion" of demons. Jesus and His disciples crossed over the lake and sailed on to a country called Gerasenes, which was on the other side of the lake directly opposite Galilee. And so we find that when Jesus stepped out on land, a demon-possessed man from town met Jesus on the shore. Now, the Bible records that for a long time, this man had not worn any clothes. For a long time, this man had not lived in a house. For a long time, this man had lived in isolation. For a long time, this man had lived among the dead. For a long time, this man had lived among the tombs. For a long time, this man had live in the cemetery. How many of you know that my "long time" and your "long time" are not the same. A "long time" is a matter of perspective!

For a long time, some of us have been praying for a breakthrough. For a long time, some of us have been hoping for a miracle. For a long time, some of us have asked, "How long Lord, how long?" For a long time, some of us have been working toward a goal. For a long time, many of us have been waiting on God to move. For a long time, some of us have not understood that God's timing is not our timing. For a long time, many of us have not known which way to turn. For a long time, many of us have been waiting for our deliverance.

But this demon-possessed man, when he saw Jesus, cried out in a loud voice. This man, so badly in need of deliverance, when he saw Jesus, shouted out at the top of his lungs, *What do you want with me, Jesus? You are the Son of the Most High God! I beg you, do not torture me. Go away and leave me alone. I know who you are. I know what you can do!* I know that if this man wants deliverance, if this man prays for deliverance, if this man cries out for deliverance, I know God well enough to know that He will deliver him! It is interesting to me that the demonic spirit in the man knew that if the man (not the spirit) would cry out to the Lord, that the Lord would deliver him.

Even though the demoniac was in a graveyard, he was not dead. He was living among the dead, but he was not dead. So he still had a chance for new life. The enemy made one mistake. He left the demoniac half-dead! And anything that is half-dead is half-alive! And so I will take that half of me that is yet alive and call out to Jesus.

What we fail to realize is that peace is not simply the absence of conflict. Just because I don't hear gunfire does not mean that we are not at war. Peace is not just the absence of the sounds of war. I heard a preacher say that you can be silent and still be in rebellion. Peace is the presence of reconciliation. Where there is no reconciliation, there is no peace! Reckon the old thing to be dead and let God do a new thing with a spirit and heart toward reconciliation. Simply because God is able to deliver, God is able to set free and God is able to make all things new again! God is able!

Simply surrender the stronghold to God and wait for Him to work a miracle in your life. What is a stronghold? It is that thing, that situation and that set of circumstances that keep holding you back. There must be no fear when it comes to facing and reconciling strongholds. Whenever we are caught up in life, one has to be strong enough and aggressive enough not to just pull, but to snatch someone out of a dangerous situation.

It is God and only God who is strong and aggressive enough to snatch us out of the kingdom of darkness. He grabs us by the back of our necks and snatches us out of danger, just in the nick of time. He grabs us back with His passion, grabs us back when we call Him and grabs us back, just in the nick of time. He rescues us because it is His desire that none of us would perish, but that we would all come into the knowledge and the saving power of Jesus Christ our Lord.

Now, this is the assurance I wish for you to take from these words: God Almighty is the only one I know to be strong enough and aggressive enough to deliver us from every life-threatening, dangerous situation in our lives. And through the finished work of God's Son, our Elder Brother, Jesus Christ, on a hill called Calvary, God can and God will deliver you and He will deliver me! I don't care what the situation might be, God can and God will deliver.

Down through the ages, God has left us with the testimonies of a faithful few who know for themselves that God is Deliverer, Savior, Strong Tower, Refuge, Protector, Lord, King, Counselor. Where are my witnesses? Paul says, *If He was strong enough to save a murderous zealot like me, I know He can save you.* Daniel says, *If He was big enough to rescue me first from a fiery furnace and then from a lion's den, I know He can deliver you too.* A grateful leper says, *If He was strong enough to heal me from the physical legions of my infirmities and the psychological scares of isolation, scorn and ridicule then I know He can and will deliver you.* Lazarus says, *If He was powerful enough to raise my bandaged up smelly body from the dead, then I am quite sure He can and will deliver you.* Mary Magdalene says, *If He was compassionate enough to forgive my adulterous mess and cover me when they wanted to stone me, then I know He will cover you too.* Peter says, *If he was understanding enough not to reject me when I denied Him and ran away from Him after all He had done for me, sit on the shore and eat fish we couldn't have caught without Him and then restore me, then I know He will not reject you.* Rahab says, *If He was gracious enough to wash me, cleanse me and purify me when I was not living like my body was the temple of the Holy Ghost, then I know God will (in the name of Jesus) do the same for you.*

All I have to do is hold on! All I have to do is hang in there! All I have to do is praise Him in the middle of it!

Then you can tell the world and everybody who said that it would never happen, by this, I know the Lord favors me. For He has not allowed my enemies to triumph over me!

Is there anybody who is willing to confess to God that you need deliverance from something? Is there anybody who can testify that drug addicts aren't the only ones who need deliverance? Is there anybody who can testify that alcoholics aren't the only ones who need deliverance? Prostitutes, adulterers, fornicators, liars, gossipers, backbiters, robbers, rapists, aren't the only ones who need deliverance! Let me tell you who else might need deliverance. Church folk need deliverance! Bible-toting saints need deliverance! Tongue-talking saints need deliverance! Scripture-reading, scripture-memorizing saints need deliverance! The ushers, the greeters the armor bearers and security need deliverance. The deacons, the trustees and the ministry leaders need deliverance! The faithful member needs deliverance. The bench warmer needs deliverance! The tither and the miser need deliverance! The drummer needs deliverance! The bass player needs deliverance! The organist, the keyboardist, the soprano, the alto, the tenor and the bass singer need deliverance.

Uh-oh, here we go! The preacher might need deliverance! The pastor just might need deliverance! Your bishop might need deliverance! Your State Mother might need deliverance! Your moderator, the president, the district supervisor and your presiding prelate just might need deliverance! Everybody needs deliverance from something! Everybody needs the hand of God to set us free from something. From the pulpit to the parking lot, everybody needs deliverance of some kind in one area or another! By the word of God and the power of His might, I'm going to lay hold of mine right now. I believe that my deliverance, my blessing, my breakthrough, my healing, is all on the way!

And if you believe that your deliverance is on the way, let the redeemed of the Lord say so! Say that you're healed! Say that you have been made whole! Say that you're set free! Say that you are delivered! Hallelujah!

# CHAPTER 7

# God Will Remember

*Paul, an apostle of Jesus Christ by the will of God, according to the promise of life which is in Christ Jesus, To Timothy, my dearly beloved son: Grace, mercy, and peace, from God the Father and Christ Jesus our Lord. I thank God, whom I serve from my forefathers with pure conscience, that without ceasing I have remembrance of thee in my prayers night and day; Greatly desiring to see thee, being mindful of thy tears, that I may be filled with joy; When I call to remembrance the unfeigned faith that is in thee, which dwelt first in thy grandmother Lois, and thy mother Eunice; and I am persuaded that in thee also. Wherefore I put thee in remembrance that thou stir up the gift of God, which is in thee by the putting on of my hands. For God hath not given us the spirit of fear; but of power, and of love, and of a sound mind. Be not thou therefore ashamed of the testimony*

*of our Lord, nor of me his prisoner: but be thou partaker of the afflictions of the gospel according to the power of God; Who hath saved us, and called us with an holy calling, not according to our works, but according to his own purpose and grace, which was given us in Christ Jesus before the world began, But is now made manifest by the appearing of our Savior Jesus Christ, who hath abolished death, and hath brought life and immortality to light through the gospel.* —2Timothy 1:1-10

*W*hatever happened to authenticity in preaching? Whatever happened to preachers who did not mind, and were not afraid to do what my Big Mama called standing flat-footed and preaching the unadulterated Word of God? There were no hidden agendas, no power plays, no words of pundits and critics, no words of experts, pretenders or so-called movers and shakers that took precedence over or were more important than *Thus saith the Lord Our God to His people.* There appears to be no shortage of preachers who place ambition over anointing, who place man's position over God's power, who place the world's goodies over God's grace, materialism over mercy, the quick fix over God's favor and microwave solutions over the long-lasting miracles of God.

I agree with Phillip Brooks who, at Yale University in 1877 in his Lyman Beecher lectures, stated, "Preaching is the bringing of truth through personality." Yet, preaching, and quite possibly pastoring, in these last and evil days has taken on another kind of personality. It has taken on the overpowering attribute of charisma. Now let me be clear, charisma does give one the ability to draw, yet not the ability to transform. It takes more than a suit and a smile, a robe and a smile, a collar and a smile, a super-sized metal cross and a thick, dangling, gold-plated chain to transform the hearts and the minds of people. There is no shortage of preaching that is not necessarily assessed on the strength of the Word, but on the size of the allotment of the trait called charisma.

Preaching has clothed itself in another agenda. However, we've got to have more than charisma. We must have more than personality. We must speak with holy authenticity. We must proclaim the Word of God with much tenacity. We must preach as Jesus did with an eloquent, yet powerful simplicity. We must maintain a sense of divine respectability. We must craft our sermons with ingenuity and creativity. Yes, we've got to have more than charisma! We need God's truth: that truth of the Gospel, that truth that binds and loosens, that truth that frees and liberates! That beautiful truth that saves and delivers, that truth that opens a wound, cleans a wound, closes a wound and then heals a wound, that truth that makes you run and makes you dance, that's a truth that lifts and separates.

It's more than charisma! Charisma is that thing that draws people to you. Charisma is that    attribute that brings them in, but only the truth will keep them in. Preachers who merely have charisma have no power to confront evil and no power to tear down strongholds. It takes more than charisma; I need passion for what I do. I need power to do what I do! I need to know that more than a superficial, illusive objective, there is a holy and divine purpose in the details of what I do. Every preacher should give utterance to God's truth in his or her own way, through his or her own personality.  No two pastors are alike! No two preachers are alike! Every branch of Zion is different, unique in the sight of God.

When Paul wrote this salutation to young Timothy, he was sitting in a Roman prison. By the time Paul wrote this letter to Timothy, his conditions had changed. He was literally bound in a dungeon expecting to die. He had been judged and sentenced to be executed and he was living his final days in prison. Paul was to die not by crucifixion, not by lethal injection, not by electrocution, but Paul was to be beheaded. Paul knew that in just a few days, the Roman soldiers would come to his cell, put him chains and take him to his place of execution.

But while Paul was waiting, he received a letter from young Timothy. While reading Timothy's letter, Paul perceived that Timothy, as a young leader in the church, was in trouble. Paul knew what Timothy was going through and realized from personal experience and from reading the words of the young pastor that a spirit of fear was taking residence in Timothy due to the fact that persecution was sweeping through the church like wildfire. Timothy was fighting feelings of hurt and devastation because the leaders he had trusted had abandoned him in this hour of great need. Paul encouraged Timothy to be bold in representing Jesus! Paul explained that God did not give us a spirit of fear, but of power, of love and of a sound mind! Paul knew about the hardships of Christian service and especially Christian leadership!

Paul compared Christians to soldiers who live to please their commanding officer. He compared them to athletes who must follow the rules, discipline and train their bodies if they expect to win the prize. He compared them to farmers who work hard, have patience and receive a great harvest. I'd like to add another comparison to this list: fishermen, who rise early, work long hours, cast their nets and still quite possibly catch nothing, but nonetheless allow Christ to translate those skills and become fishers of men. I'd like to include pastors who take calls in the

110

middle of the night to rescue the critical and the chronic, the distraught and the suicidal.

Paul knew what this was like because, as he explained to Timothy in Chapter 4:16, he had had similar experiences. The Apostle Paul makes it clear that at one of the lowest points in his life, he, too, had been abandoned. *At my first trial, at my first defense no one was with me to support me, but all abandoned me. But don't hold it against them; it's all right. The Lord stood with me and empowered me that as His spirit is working through me the Gospel of Jesus Christ might be fully accomplished and all of the Gentiles might hear what Good News our Lord has wrought upon those who have an ear to hear it. I was fully delivered out of the lion's mouth.* It is only through the Gospel that real Good News of Jesus Christ that we can be fully delivered! Not partially delivered, but fully delivered. Not delivered today and down tomorrow, but fully delivered! Paul had quite a bit of advice for Timothy in this second letter. He told him to pursue righteousness, faith, love, and peace. Join in with the other cloud of witnesses! Call on God, Timothy, just as they do out of a pure heart!

Don't have anything to do with foolish and stupid arguments because all they do is produce quarrels. He said, *Think it not strange son, the last days are coming and there will be signs to look for.* People will be lovers of themselves, lovers of money, boastful, proud, abusive, disobedient to their parents, ungrateful, unholy, without love, unforgiving, slanderous, without self-control, brutal, not lovers of good, treacherous, rash, conceited, lovers of pleasure rather than lovers of God, having a form of godliness but denying its power. Does this not sound like the world we love in today? No matter what the situation or the condition of the people, Paul tells Timothy to preach, be ready for any opportunity and simply run on and see what the end is going to be!

Paul, the pastor, knew that young Timothy needed encouraging and he might not get this chance again, so he wrote back to Timothy and, after a proper salutation, he said, *I thank God, whom I serve from my forefathers with pure conscious, that without ceasing I have remembrance of you in my prayers, night and day...* How about that? The pastor is in trouble and yet he's not asking anyone to pray for him, he is telling somebody else, "I thank God that I have the awesome opportunity to pray for you. As I remember you, I pray for you."

It is written that the word 'remember' or 'remembrance' comes from a Greek word that means a written record used to record and to memorialize a person's actions. In a few other places in the Bible, to remember means to be represented by a statue, a monument or a memorial. But one of the most interesting definitions of 'remember' means "to have and to hold." What does all of this have to do with Paul's prayer for Timothy? As Paul prayed for Timothy, I believe that he wanted heaven to remember the record of service that Timothy was giving unto the Kingdom. So that if Timothy just happened to stumble while in the service of the Lord, he wanted heaven to remember all he had done to lift up the name of Jesus and expand the Kingdom of God. Before Paul lifted up the needs of Timothy, he lifted up, remembered, called to mind, did a roll call, and took the time to tell heaven just how he felt about the young apostle.

Paul memorialized Timothy's record and heart of service before the Lord. Paul recalled Timothy's acts of faith in the name of Jesus. Paul recalled Timothy's acts of defiance in the face of danger and he did it all for the building up of the Kingdom of God. Paul understood that the effectual fervent prayers of the righteous would make a whole lot of things available, turn impossible situations around, and make people do what they said they would never do not by charisma, but through prayer

It takes more than charisma to heal a broken heart and mend a wounded soul; charisma will draw, but may not transform. I have found that God's passion, power, and purpose will mend hearts and change lives. A good preacher or a caring and compassionate pastor possesses these characterizing life-changing qualities; and when you operate out of the great limitless storehouse of God and you invest in the lives of the people (the citizens of the Kingdom of God) memories of your good work in the Kingdom will be lasting. Therefore, the people will testify about the love of Christ you showed them in their time of need. The people will rejoice in your holy regard for the issues of their lives and the faith you helped renew when life threw them a curve ball. This is how they will remember you and thank you for your servant's heart:

- I remember, Pastor, when you eulogized my mother, my father and other loved ones, and I thank God, the God whom I serve, for you.

- I remember when you visited me when I was sick and I thank God for your compassion.

- I remember, Pastor, when you lifted me up when everybody else put me down and I want to thank the God I serve for you.

- I remember the precious time you gave me; stopped what you were doing and carved out of your busy schedule a few moments just for me and right now, I just want to thank the God that I serve for you.

- I remember the prayers you prayed for me when I couldn't pray for myself and I want to thank the God I serve for you.

- I remember when you counseled me out of depression, counseled me out of suicide, talked me out of giving up, wouldn't let me throw in the towel and I just want to thank the God I serve for you.

- I remember how you endured sickness in your own body and how your life served as an example for the way a child of God must suffer and goes through with dignity.

- I remember when you endured pain in his own heart, yet you still had enough God in you to bind up the brokenhearted.

- I remember when I was broken before God and your words gave me comfort!

- I remember when I had backslidden, messed up, my life all jacked up and I needed to rededicate my life to Christ. Pastor, your word gave me the encouragement I needed to come back to the Lord!

- I remember when I faced one of the greatest challenges of my life, thank you pastor you prayed for me and God gave me strength!

I thank God for pastors and preachers after God's own heart. I thank God for the called and chosen men and women of the Kingdom who thought it not robbery to sow into my life, to encourage my heart, to listen to my heart more than my words and my laments, to take the time to calm my fears and dry my tears. I thank God that spiritual fathers and mothers took the time to help me understand that God has not forgotten, God sees, God knows and all of it, EVERYTHING, will work together for my good. It's not the isolative nature of each situation on its own that will mature you, but it is the working together, the synergistic nature of the good, the bad and the ugly that is preparing you for greater works, a greater anointing and yes, even greater sacrifice!

God knows every disappointment and every discouragement a preacher may face, but he has given the committed ones an attitude that says, "I will preach what the Word says." This kind of attitude surpasses charisma. God has given genuine pastors an "I've got to love you any way" personality. This kind of personality surpasses charisma.

God knows every burden of a pastor's heart for those folk who are lost and on their way to hell, and God will remember, long after the charisma is gone, the preachers and pastors who are faithful to the Word and to His service.

# CHAPTER 8

# Thank God for What Didn't Happen

*O give thanks unto the* LORD, *for he is good: for his mercy endureth for ever. Let the redeemed of the* LORD *say so, whom he hath redeemed from the hand of the enemy; And gathered them out of the lands, from the east, and from the west, from the north, and from the south. They wandered in the wilderness in a solitary way; they found no city to dwell in. Hungry and thirsty, their soul fainted in them. Then they cried unto the* LORD *in their trouble, and he delivered them out of their distresses.* — Psalm 107

*W*ell, here we are again on the cusp of another breakthrough; another move of God and each of us finds ourselves wondering how in the world we made it through. Sometimes, there is nothing else to say but thank you Jesus! At the end of a season of struggle when at times it has felt like all out warfare, I'm tired and my energy has been spent fighting back the hounds of hell that would (if they could) destroy everything that I've worked for, prayed for, cried and travailed over. With that having been said, all I want to say is, "Thank you, Jesus!"

If you have been preaching for a while, you understand that one literally struggles around this time of the year to craft a sermon that is new and fresh and has something to add to this season of reflection and thanksgiving. We're trying to avoid the clichés, the tried and true adages that we hear every year. Pastors want to tell you something that you haven't heard before, seeking to deliver a new revelation on an old theme.

However, I believe that in this rapidly changing world where the new phone you just purchased already has an upgrade waiting in the wing, if you have purchased the current version of windows, the new adaptation is waiting in the wings before the ink is dry on the receipt. For the God chaser and the Jesus lover, and all champions of the Gospel, the old news is still good news.

Therefore, in this season of breakthroughs, I won't change the tradition of preaching what is truly a manifesto for grateful people. I will just try to show you a side you may not have considered. I'm not going to move and take the easy way out, but we are going to take our time and bless the name of the Lord. For the Bible simply declares, *O Give thanks unto the Lord because He is good.* He's good! That's easily identifiable; He's good. It is highly recognizable when we see the goodness of the Lord. It's easy to give God thanks for the blessings. Blessings are good; they give us joy, make us feel good and are the manifested answers to our prayers. When life is good and all is well it is easy to lift our voices, shout hallelujah, talk about all the ways God has made and about all of the doors He has opened. It's easy to reminisce about the healings God sent, the unexpected check that came in the mail and the miraculous cancelation of that debt that made you pace the floor night after night. It's easy to remember how God shut the devil's mouth, and made a liar and a thief out of Satan on your behalf.

It's good to remember how He bought books, paid tuition, helped you pass tests, and wouldn't let the sleepy demon overtake you when you needed to stay up all night and study. I get a "hallelujah high" when I just stop for a moment in the heat of the battle and thank God for being

119

a promise keeper, a burden bearer, a heavy load sharer, a confidant, a healer, a heart fixer, and a mind regulator.

I get Jesus joy when I think about the fact that He never fails (He's good), is never early (He's good), is never ever late (that's better), but always right on time (that's the absolute best). When Jesus comes, He comes with healing in his wings; He brings the right prescription, appropriate medication, the most accurate diagnosis, and proper prognosis. He's Dr. Jesus, the perfect general practitioner, specializing in every illness, every disease, every malady, every disorder, every condition, curing the incurable, defying medical research, and demystifying medical mysteries, disappointing cancer and dissolving tumors. Why? He's all wise, omnipotent (all-powerful), omniscient (all knowing), omnipresent (everywhere at the same time), all knowing (He's good). My God and your God is altogether lovely!

There are those of us who are so grateful that we serve the only wise God, that when we think about the goodness of Jesus, and all He has done, is doing and will do in our lives, I don't know about your soul, but my soul shouts, cries, testifies, and bears witness to the hallelujah of the saints. I thank God for blessing me.

Yet, I propose that there is another side to the gratitude that we rarely think about. There is another side to the appreciation that we forget to thank God for. I want to take the time to reveal something that you already know in your spirit and believe in your heart, but may not have confessed with your mouth. Stop right now, and don't forget to thank God for what didn't happen.

While you're thanking God for how He blessed, delivered and healed you, just imagine for a moment what it would have been like if God had not come to your rescue. Reminisce for just a minute what it would have been like if God did not show up on time. What it would have been like if God had not prepared a table before you in front of your enemies. Whether you are in a struggle, just coming out of a struggle or headed into a struggle, PLEASE DON'T FORGET TO THANK GOD FOR WHAT DID NOT HAPPEN!

Put this book down for one minute, and take time to thank God for what did not happen. Turn that one sentence into a testimony service like this, "I want to thank God for what did not happen to me between my bondage and my deliverance. The devil thought he had me, but I got away! I want to thank God for what did not happen!"

Can you think of just one place in your life where the devil re-used his ugly head and thought he won? If so, then you ought to put your hands together and thank God for what did not happen. Can you think of at least one situation where your friends, your family, your roommate, your enemies, your haters, your agitators thought you were down for the count, but just when they thought it was over, God showed up and you stood back up before the fight could be called a technical knockout? If so, I strongly suggest you make some noise and thank God for what did not happen. Well, if you can't tell it, let me tell what the Lord didn't let happen to me:

- I thank God for the disease that did not happen.
- I thank God for the accident that did not happen.
- I thank God for the sickness that did not happen.
- I thank God for the hurricane that did not happen.
- I thank God for the lies that didn't kill me.
- I thank God for the gossip that didn't hurt me.
- I thank God for the betrayal that didn't fatally wound me.
- I thank God for the friends who did not leave me.
- I thank God for the Son who didn't give up.
- I thank God for the confidence I did not lose.
- I thank God for the momentum that did not disappear.
- I thank God for the tragedy that didn't happen.
- I thank God that you did not give me some of the things I asked you for.

• I thank God that I didn't get my way, because it was the wrong way.

Okay, it's your turn now! I thank you, God, that in spite of everything I've been through I didn't lose my way! It didn't happen. I didn't lose my praise! It didn't happen. I didn't lose my dance! Thank you, God, for what didn't happen! Thank you God for the STD you didn't contract. Thank you for the HIV or AIDS that didn't happen! Thank you for the stray bullet that did not hit you when you were in the wrong place at the wrong time. Thank you for the fight that didn't happen. I thank you for the date rape that didn't happen. I thank you for the alcohol poisoning that didn't happen.

Psalm 107 is a Psalm of testimonies about where God showed up in the life of the Psalmist. Psalm 107 is about desperate situations that continuously show up in people's lives, not just in the Old Testament, but also in the 21st Century.

I read somewhere that the Pilgrims, those early settlers that landed on Plymouth Rock, were in trouble and just about to perish in the wilderness, when they had the good sense to cry out to the Lord. I read somewhere that Psalm 107 was a favorite psalm of the Pilgrims. He heard their voices and saved them from their troubles. They prayed, thanking God for the bounty and for preserving them in a harsh and unforgiving land. I believe that maybe, just maybe, a part of their prayer was that they thanked God for what did not happen!

Let's take a clue from Psalm 107:2 that simply says, *Let the redeemed of the Lord say!* You ought to say so on today! If he brought you back, you ought to say so! If he rescued you, you ought to say so! If he has taken care of you, you ought to say so! If the Lord has kept you, you ought to say so! If the Lord has blessed you, you ought to say so!

Why must I say so? I've got to say so because I can't disengage from my praise. My life depends on my praise. My success depends on my praise. My happiness depends on my praise. My joy and my safety depend on my praise. My salvation and my eternal destination depend on my confession, my proclamation and my praise.

I'm studying to be a doctor, but my success in the operation room is in my praise. I'm studying to be a lawyer, but my success in the courtroom depends on my praise. I'm studying to be an architect, but whatever I design will be a product of my praise. I'm studying to become an educator, scientist, politician, psychologist, counselor, tycoon, entrepreneur, CEO, it does not matter because my success will come out of my praise, and I'll praise God for what did not happen, just as hard for what did happen.

Why? I'll praise Him for what did not happen because every opened door isn't from God. Not every lifted window will lead you to a better future. Thank God for closed doors, locked windows, and blocked roads. How does praise rise up in your spirit? An individual experiences a crisis and something on the inside compels him or her to give thanks to God for deliverance from that crisis. Crisis is an opportunity to trust God or give in to the devil (danger). The opportunity is in the crisis, while the crisis presents the opportunity. When I cry out to God, that's a crisis in progress (that's my trouble). When I give thanks to God for what He has done, that's a crisis that has passed (it's my testimony) and when I praise God, my praise is the grateful product of my escape from the crisis (that's my worship).

Therefore, when they ask me what I'm grateful for, I will tell them I'm grateful for the experience, grateful for the crisis, but more than anything, I'm grateful for the opportunity to tell somebody that I thank God for what did not happen. How do I know it didn't happen? I'm still here, to give God glory. I'm still here to give God honor, and I'm still here to give God praise.

I am living proof that God is my help. I am the living proof that I survived, made it over, persisted, didn't give up, wouldn't let go and kept holding on.

I want to thank God for what did not happen!

# SERMONIC STORIES: MOVEMENT III

## Restoration

*I will praise you; for I am fearfully and wonderfully made: marvelous are your works; and that my soul knows so well.* — Psalm 139:14

$\mathcal{I}$n the living room of my childhood home, there is a beautiful Duncan Phyfe style sofa with carved woodworks and claw feet upholstered in tapestry. This classic piece of furniture has been in our family for quite some time. Many things have changed in that room over the years however, that sofa has remained. Just one look at it and you will conclude that according to the design, the carvings, the stately symmetry of the nail work and the sturdiness of the frame, its designer and manufacturer was careful in its making.

Nevertheless, however beautiful this period piece was (circa 1930), you could not help but notice that this dearly beloved heirloom needed some restoration. The wood needed a little retouching, the padding needed replacing and new upholstery needed to be selected. You could also tell, just by observation, that this sofa was not a victim of abuse or misuse; it had not been mishandled or broken, cut or torn. It simply had become worn due to the pressures of life and the everyday activities of a family gathering to read, to pray, to laugh, the entertain, to rest and quite simply to live. Life had happened to our sofa.

The upholstery of this sofa is much like the fabric of our lives — worn and a bit tired looking on the outside, but our true integrity depends upon what lies on the inside. According to the furniture restorer, the sofa had retained wholeness and soundness in its inner parts. The frame was solid and the hand-tied springs were in near impeccable condition. Such as it is in life — in the hands of the right person — the Master Restorer, the one who specializes in the work of restoration, renovation, renewal, redemption, recovery, rescue, reformation, reclamation and revival. ALL THINGS CAN BECOME NEW!

Whether it is a life, a ministry, a marriage, a partnership, or a friendship, we must know that God specializes in the work of restoration! I can count it all joy because God makes everything new! If He did it for me, and He did, He can and will do it for you, and He will. God restored my joy; restored my peace; restored my faith in people; gave me my life back just so that I could offer it back to him as a living sacrifice for all He has done for me. And guess what? It's still not enough! Praise the Lord, everybody! We are fearfully and wonderfully made! I am, thank you Jesus, living in the beautiful state of restoration! What about you? Hallelujah!

# CHAPTER 9

# Count It All Joy!

*My brethren, count it all joy when you fall into divers temptations; Knowing this: that the trying of your soul worketh patience. But let patience have her perfect work, that you may be perfect and entire, wanting nothing.* —James 1:2-4

$\mathscr{I}$ am always amazed that the more I study the life of Jesus, the more I attempt to learn about Jesus, the more I desire to know His way and the more I think I have begun to figure out the complexity of the One whose Gospel was so uncomplicated, the more I am convinced that this same

Jesus is the most significant figure to ever grace the stage of this great life-sustaining planet we call Earth.

I believe it is the strength of His character, the level of His commitment and the depth of His conviction that makes the saving knowledge of Jesus Christ of Nazareth inexhaustible. Archaeologists cannot even find enough ancient monuments, relics and artifacts to begin to know Jesus. Paleontologists cannot dig up enough fossils to figure out Jesus. Biologists are still puzzled by the fact that He was both God and fully man. Historians did not record His birth, nor for thirty years did anyone pay much attention to His life. Christian Scientologists are still misguided by their search for the truth. Simply because the more we search the Gospel, the more Good news we find. The deeper we go, the more we are convinced that Jesus is the bottomless well of Living Water. The deeper we dig, the more there is to discover about Jesus. (Can we just talk about Jesus for a little while?)

We must remember that Jesus was born under questionable circumstances. We must remember that Jesus was the earthly son of a simple carpenter called Joseph. We must remember that Jesus was the son of a fourteen-year-old woman-child by the name of Mary. We must remember that Jesus was a country boy, a Jew from the hill country of Galilee. We must remember that Jesus showed up in Jerusalem at the age of thirty-three at the

Passover. We must remember that at the end of a three-year ministry, Jesus was arrested, tried, convicted of treason, and then executed like a common criminal by the way of the cruelest penalty of death. Jesus was crucified. Yet, in spite of all of the controversy, it is still the complexity of His personality, it is the solid rock of His Word, it is the challenge of His life that stands ever before us. It is the passion in which He pursued the mission of His Father (to save a dying world from its sins). It is the relentless pursuit of His mission to sacrifice and to serve. It is the mystery of His ministry. It is the passion with which He lived His life. And the compassion by which He served others that makes the life of Jesus absolutely riveting.

More than two thousand years later: The impact of His life is unparalleled. The impact of His life is unrivaled. The impact of His life is unequivocally unobtainable by any man's standards. In other words, ain't nobody God, but God! He never wrote a book, yet the book written about Him is the number one bestseller in the world.

It is amazing how the local ministry of Jesus became a worldwide revolution! He's Jesus: my Savior, my rock, my hiding place, my refuge, and my peace in the middle of the storm!

Hurting and wounded people sit on the pews of our church every Sunday. Feelings of failure, depression, guilt, and loneliness preoccupy the heart and the mind.

We enter the sanctuary to worship, praying and looking to find new hope for their lives and new solutions to their problems. Yet, there is healing power in the pulpit. Jesus suggests to us that we go ahead and preach good news to the poor, proclaim release to the captives, give the blind their sight back and preach liberty to those who are oppressed. However, we must also understand that brokenness is in the pulpit as well as the pew.

We were told that early to bed and early to rise makes a man healthy, wealthy and wise. But one might say, pastor, I've been going to bed early. I have been rising early, but I'm not healthier, I'm not wealthier, and it doesn't appear that I am any wiser. One might say, preacher, I have been trying to take the proverbial lemons life has handed me, and I have tried to make lemonade. But pastor sometimes the sugar jar is empty and the lemons are rotten to the core. Preacher, it's not always easy to keep your chin up and put on a happy face. It's not easy to ease on down the road. It's not easy to take Bobby McFerrin's advice when he says, "Don't worry; be happy." It's not easy preacher to smile when you feel like crying and to keep on living when you feel like dying. Life is difficult.

Situations differ from person to person, life station to life station, but the basic core of human existence is the same. We all want to be happy. We all want to live a life that is fulfilling. We all wish to make an impact on the world. It hurts preacher when bad things happen to good people. It just doesn't seem fair when good things happen to wicked people. And so we go through life with failures, frustrations, situations, circumstances, trials, tests, betrayals, heartbreak, heartache, disappointments, leavings, mourning, grieving over situations that leave us battered, broken, bruised, burned out, bewildered. The Bible teaches that man is of but a few days, and those days are full of sorrow.

However, as multi-faceted as the trials of life can be, in the midst of the mess, we can hear the voice of Jesus come through with clarion resolve beseeching us to "Come unto Me all of you who are burdened and heavy laden, and I will give you rest. Take my yoke upon you for my yoke is easy and my burden is light." In other words, "I am God, and I won't put any more on you than you can bear." In other words, "I am God and if I brought you to it, I will bring you through it. I am your God and I know the plans I have for you." In other words, "I am God; where is your faith?" In other words, "I am God! Do you not know? Have you not heard? That I am your all powerful, all knowing, all seeing God?"

As we explore this text, we find that the letters of James, Peter, John and Jude were not addressed to any specific group of believers, but were written to be applicable across many lines.

While some believe that the Book of James contains unrelated and disjointed nuggets of wisdom, I tend to believe there is a theme that ties it together. It is the theme that says when you finally realize just how blessed you are, you will find a little something called joy! The words of James reminds me of the Sermon on the Mount whereby Jesus literally sits on a mountainside and tells the people (in so many words), Listen, and don't believe the hype. I don't care what anybody else says, take my word for it, you are blessed. Children, I've come to tell you that you are blessed. I don't know about you, but I believe that I am blessed! You see if I don't believe that I'm blessed, nobody is going to believe that I'm blessed. You've got to know that come hell or high water, if God is for you, He's always more than the world against you. In the Gospel of Matthew chapter 5, Jesus preaches, "You are blessed even if you are poor in spirit, because the kingdom of heaven belongs to you." Jesus said, "You are blessed even if you mourn, because that's the time when I can send you comfort." Jesus said, "You are blessed if you are meek, for they shall inherit the earth." Jesus said, "Blessed are those who hunger and thirst after righteousness for they will be filled." Jesus said, "Blessed are the merciful, for they will receive mercy." Jesus said, "You are blessed if you have a pure heart, for you will see God." Those are the positive things. That's the good part of being blessed.

But Jesus, in his preaching, reminds the people that in this life, you are going to go through some things. You are going to have to endure some things, suffer some things, put up with some mess you don't want to put up with, deal with some folk you don't want to deal with, bite your tongue, hold back some choice words, keep from laying holy hands on a few folk. Jesus said, "I want you to remember that you are still blessed even when you are persecuted for righteousness sake; the kingdom of heaven belongs to you." Jesus said, "Blessed for you when people revile you and persecute you and utter all manner of evil against you falsely on my account." Jesus tells us to rejoice and be exceeding glad! For great is our reward in heaven! For the prophets who proceeded you were persecuted in the same way. In other words, folk who make a serious impact on the world have to go through something! And James just simply says this: Whenever you go through something, JUST COUNT IT ALL JOY!

Now this is very practical advice. He believes that our faith is made manifest in what we do; that what we believe we act on. What we believe we do; that faith in action is faith in motion. He believes that faith without action is dead religion; that it's just dead religious rhetoric. James seems to have his own mountain top experience whereby Jesus challenged his hearers, his followers and even the curious onlookers to "be perfect as your Father is perfect." How do we become perfect? Well, by the trying and the testing of our faith. How will we know how much flexibility, how much elasticity, how much durability our faith has?

The first thing I want you to consider is that a faith that cannot be tested is a faith that has not been tested. A faith that cannot be tried is a faith that cannot stand the test of time. What are you saying preacher? I'm telling you that the only way to strengthen your faith and to take strength in that faith is to practice that faith! Practice your faith if they leave your name off the bulletin. Practice your faith if they leave your name off the birthday list. Practice your faith if nobody ever calls your name. Practice your faith, if nobody ever gives you a plaque, a certificate or a gift card. Practice your faith even if…

James reminds the reader that while you are trying to do God's you will have hardships. In practicing your faith, you will be persecuted. In practicing your faith you will be cut down, you will be cast aside. Yet, it is in this practicing of your faith that James clearly and squarely shows you the theme of joy! JOY! The great theme of the Christian's life must be JOY! You find that in the opening lines of chapter one, after a proper greeting, in so many words, James says that through life amid good report and evil report, that you must "Count it all joy! COUNT IT ALL JOY! I can't go any further without a pragmatic exegesis of the hermeneutical content within this homiletical moment.

But what must I do to find that peace that passes and surpasses all understanding? Well, the first thing you must do is to do one simple thing: Simply count. What exactly do you mean by count? Well, when I count, I assign some numerical value, when I count, I add it all up, when I count, I calculate, tally, I consider the significant as well as the insignificant. I check for validity, I consider the acceptable as well as the unacceptable, when I regard, when I view, when I hold it up to the light, I can go back and say look what the Lord has done in my life. When I count, I am forced to remember what the Lord has done in my life. When I count the many blessings, when I name them one by one, I will find that God has been a faithful God! When I count my blessings and I name them one by one, I will find that God has never left me, nor has he ever forsaken me.

- When I count all my blessings and I name them one by one, I will find that God has been my strength

- When I count all my blessings and I name them one by one, I will find that God has given me power

- When I count all my blessings and I name them one by one, I will find that God is holy and sovereign

- When I count all my blessings and I name them one by one, I will find that God is forgiving and compassionate

- When I count all my blessings and I name them one by one, I will find that God is never early and never late

- When I count all my blessings and I name them one by one, I will find that God is the strength of my life.

- When I count all my blessings and I name them one by one, I will find that God is my source.

- When I count all my blessings and I name them one by one, I will find that God is my all and all.

The second observation is that we must count it! What does this word 'it' signifies? It is whatever condition you find yourself in. If you find yourself living in abundance, it is a good thing! If you find yourself in a good place in life right now, it is a good thing! If you find yourself, loving God with all of your heart, it is a good thing! If you find yourself worshiping God in spirit and in truth, it is a good thing! If you find yourself praising the Lord as if your life depends on it (God knows), that is a good thing! 'It' might be your children! 'It' might be your spouse! 'It' might be your job! 'It' might be your health! But whatever 'it' is, just COUNT IT. God is more interested in where you will end up than where you are right now. If our humiliation is necessary to bring us to our destination, then God will allow it.

The third observation is that we must count it all. How much do I count? James tells us to count it all! How much do I count? James said count it all! Every little thing, count it all! Every big thing, count it all! Every painful thing, count it all! Every difficult thing, count it all! Every lie, count it all! Every disappointment, count it all! Every betrayal, count it all! Every hardship, count it all! Every saboteur, count them all! Every backstabber, count them all! Everybody who tried to count you out, count them all! Every loss, count it all! When you filed bankruptcy, count it all! When you filed for divorce, count it all! When the business when belly up, count it all! When you lost your job, count it all! When you lost your house, count it all! When you lost your car, count it all! When you almost, I said almost, lost your mind, count it all! Every broken relationship, count it all! Every broken dream, count it all! Every missed opportunity, count it all! Every sacrifice, count it all!

The trying of your soul worketh patience. I believe James when he said, "But let patience have her perfect work, that you may be perfect and complete, wanting nothing."(James 4:1) Let patience work it out! Let patience see you through! Let patience do what folk won't do! Let patience do what only God can do! Let patience make you whole. Let patience make you perfect. Let patience make

139

you complete! Perfect in whom? Perfect in Jesus! Complete in whom? Complete in Jesus!

However, in the meantime, while I am counting, I will simply count it all joy! It's joy to know that you're blessed and highly favored of the Lord. It's joy to have the assurance that, God's goodness and His mercy will follow you everywhere that you go. I can't testify for you and you can't testify for me; all I know is that I'm glad about the joy I have found in the saving power of Jesus Christ! How about you? Are you glad about it? Are you glad about his joy! Are you glad that He saved you? Are you glad that He raised you? Are you glad that God looked beyond all of your faults and saw your needs? I pray that you're glad about that joy that the world did not give you. It's that same joy that the world cannot take away.

I don't care about what you have been through; it's still joy! I don't care what it looks like; it's still joy! I don't care what it feels like; it is still joy! I don't care if it left a bitter taste in your mouth; it's still joy! It didn't make me happy, but I still got my joy! I had to cry sometimes, but I've still got my joy! I've had to bit my tongue, turn my head, let you insult me, let you disrespect me, let you lie on me, let you betray me, but guess what, I'VE…STILL…GOT…MY…JOY!

# CHAPTER 10

# Praise the Lord, Everybody!

*Let everything that has breath, praise the Lord! Praise ye the Lord!* —Psalm 150

Deacon Mack Williams, Deacon Tom Johnson, Deacon Lewis Davis, Deacon James L. Brown, Deacon William Dwight, Deacon Franklin Banks, Deacon Frank Cutter, Sis. Rusie Evans, Mother Mattie Bell Williams, Sister Eloise Williams, Sister Flora Bell Lewis, Sister Mavis Brown, Sister Ella Mae Davis, Sister Fannie Tarver, Reverend F. J. Roundtree, Rev. Thomas Sapp, Reverend C. J. Walker, Reverend Scott Jackson, Sister Alma Clarke, Mother

Wardie Adams, The Lula Tarver Missionary Circle #1, The Baptist Training Union, The Walker Baptist Association and on and on and on. These names are unfamiliar to you, but they all mean so much to me. These are just a few names that were instrumental in my spiritual growth and development. I would not trade these people or my small town beginnings for anything but heaven. I would not trade the reality that I grew up in a small town where long rectangular tables outside of small country churches were filled with the best food at church anniversaries and homecoming, pastors' anniversaries, women's days, men's days and youth church celebrations! It wasn't anniversary unless you took a plate home from everybody's basket and fixed more plates right out the trunk of the saints' cars. But even with all of those long tables and big baskets there was barely enough room for all of the food. You had to be there to understand.

There were old-fashioned revivals, the lining of hymns by deacons who sat in the "Amen Corner," choir anniversaries, quartet singings, Gospel Pearls songbooks, missionary meetings, prayer meetings, tent revivals, fish fries, Easter egg hunts. I can remember the Sunday school picnics and the fact that my sister and I could count how many times we missed Sunday school on one hand and still have some fingers left over. I remember Watch Night service, Easter Sunrise service, and outdoor baptismal pools.

I remember that families took turns cleaning and taking care of the church. We cleaned the building, and cut grass, mopped floors, cleaned sinks and toilets, scrubbed base boards, cut grass or (mowed the lawn) trimmed hedges, painted walls, washed dishes, set tables, vacuumed, dusted, peeled potatoes, made salad, peeled eggs, fried chicken, and fixed plates. You name it; we did it! We did it all unto the glory of the Lord!

I did not realize it then, but I came to realize that everything we did — all of the work done — was not about us, but it was about God! It was about worship! It was about the fact that this Christian walk was not about how much power we could wield, but how much service we could give. It was about asking and answering the song, "What shall I render unto God for all His blessings? What shall I render? Tell me, what shall I give? Since God has everything and everything belongs to Him? Tell me what shall I give? That question is answered in Psalm 150. The writer says, *Let everything that has breath praise the Lord!* In everything that I do, I'm going to give God the glory! In everything and in all things I am going to give my God the glory and give my God the praise! That is to say that if I'm singing in the choir, I'm going to give Him praise! If I am a deacon, while I'm serving, I'll worship Him in spirit and in truth! If I am a minister of the gospel, while I'm delivering His Word, I will worship Him because he has anointed me to bring good tidings of great joy to the nations and with every Holy Ghost inspired word, I will worship Him. If I am an usher, my spirit will lead the spirit of every parishioner to enter His gates with thanksgiving and enter His courts with praise! In whatever post I hold, I will worship Him. In my giving, I will worship! In my living, I will worship! In my serving, I will worship!

But it was the testimony service where the clarion call was issued for somebody, anybody to get up and get ready to give a testimony of praise! And like clockwork, some happy saint, some hilarious saint, some glad-to-be-in-the-number, glad-to-be-in-the-service saint who did not have a mike but would set the testimony service off with these words: "First giving honor to God and to my Lord and Savior, Jesus Christ, Who is the head of my life and the author and the finisher of my faith. It is indeed an honor and a privilege to be able to stand in the house of the Lord one more time and give praise to His high and holy name. It is a name that is above every name. At the name of Jesus, every knee shall bow and every tongue shall confess that Jesus is Lord! I want to thank God for life, health, and strength. I want to thank God for keeping me all night long while I slumbered and I slept. I want to thank God and praise Him, too, because when I lifted my eyes this morning I did not lift them in hell. I want to thank God this morning that my tongue was not fastened to the roof of my mouth. I want to thank God that my bed sheets did not become my winding sheets. I want to thank God that my nightclothes did not become my grave clothes! I want to thank God that my mattress and my box spring did not become my cooling board in an undertaker's closet. I want to thank God this morning that I'm still in the land of the living!

Saints, I just want you to know that I'm praying that your faith would increase, that your joy would overflow, that your love would be ever abounding and that the name and the praises of Jesus will forever be on your lips and the love of God will overtake your heart! Church, I'm running for my life and I've got heaven in my view! Now as I take my seat, I want all of you to pray for me, as I pray for you! And whatever you do, don't forget to just to keep on praising the Lord, everybody! Praise the Lord!" And the people would shout hallelujah! The organ would join in, the drummer would catch on, the guitar player would strum out a bass line and the whole church would be in a state of holy chaos! Now I don't know how you feel about this little trip down memory lane, but I know that the mandate is still the same, Let everything that has breath, praise the Lord!

It is in this light that we find that the Psalms are full of commands to praise the Lord! We find that in the Psalms each writer expresses many of the feelings and emotions we experience in life. We find that the psalmists express their emotions, talk to God, cry out to God, give praise and worship to God, turn their enemies over to God, give thanks unto God, claim victory by the power of God and give all that they are and all they hope to be to God. These psalmists share their joy and sorrow, their discouragement and thanksgiving, their pain and the heartache, their fears and their worries, their shortcomings and their failures, their fears of enemies and death, the need for forgiveness and the downfall of sin, how God can rescue people from danger and answer the cries of a people from slavery and oppression.

Psalm 150 is a strong reminder that worship is not about us, but that worship is about God. Worship is about the God who created both the heavens and the earth. We must remember that this same God who has given us breath is now requesting that we take this same breath and use it to give Him praise. Psalm 150 is a command. It is an imperative statement that leaves no room for discussion.

Psalm 150 commands that we simply…worship! In verses 1 through 5, we receive a string of commands, eleven imperative commands. But it is only until we reach the end of verse 6 that we are told who is being commanded to praise the Lord. Who is to praise the Lord? Everything that breathes upon this earth is to praise the Lord!

The writers of these psalms brought everything to God. But here in this 150th Psalm is a message of pure praise from the beginning to the end. Thirteen times it calls on us and all living creatures to just praise the Lord!

Psalm 150 reminds us that no matter what is going on in our lives, we must remember to praise God for His faithfulness in our lives.

Everybody is supposed to praise the Lord. When God breathed life into the nostrils of Adam, man became a living soul. Now, here in Psalm 150, God commands us to take that same breath and give it back to him in praise and in worship.

However, this Holy Ghost praise party does not begin with Psalm 150, but if we would just step back for a few verses, we will find that Psalm 145 calls us to worship the greatness of God, and that He is most worthy of all glory and honor. It tells us to meditate on His awesome power and all of the things that He has done. It's not what you want Him to do, but what He has done. It's what He has brought you through; what He has kept you from; what He has delivered you from; how He has blessed you in the face of your enemies; how He has already shut the devil's mouth; how He made every one of your enemies your footstool; how He has raised you up.

The command is that we are to praise Him for the mighty works of His hands! Praise him for the wind and the rain! Praise Him for the new mercies we receive every day. We are invited to Praise Him because we could have been dead if He had not kept us. In fact, when I think of the goodness of Jesus and all He has done for me, my soul cries out "Hallelujah! I thank God for blessing me!" We can praise Him because He is a gracious God, slow to anger, abounding in love and faithfulness. We can praise Him because He looks at us all through the eyes of compassion and love. We can praise Him because when we should have received justice, He gave us mercy! When we should have received justice, He gave us grace! And when we think on these things, we realize just how much we have to proclaim about the goodness of the Lord. When we think on these things, we must certainly bless His high holy name.

In addition, Psalm 146 reminds us that we must praise our Maker! The last five Psalms all begin and end with these words: Praise the Lord! In Hebrew, these words, "Praise the Lord" simply translate to the word, "Hallelujah!" This Psalm begins with the psalmist's determination that whatever was going on in his life, he was going to keep on praising God for as long as he lived. Like the psalmist, I'm going to praise Him because He is worthy to be praised. I'm going to praise Him because I can trust Him! I'm going to praise Him, because I can count on Him! I'm going to praise Him because I appreciate Him! I'm going to praise Him because I am powerless in the face of Him! I'm going to praise Him because I am strong because of Him! I'm going to praise Him, because all of my plans come to nothing without Him! I'm going to praise Him because I have no purpose in life apart from Him! I'm going to praise Him because all of my help comes from Him! I'm going to praise Him because there is no shadow of turning in Him!

There is no joy without God. There is no love apart from Him! There are no limits to His power, no limits to His compassion! And for all of His goodness and all of His mercy, what does He ask of us? No, what does he command us to do? He commands us to give Him the praise. Why? Well, it is because my praise is accompanied by the assurance that if I praise Him, He'll provide for all of my needs! If I praise Him, He will encourage my heart; order my steps and secure my life; put running in my feet; clapping in my hands; give me a song in the night; meet me in my secret closet; answer my prayers; let me live off of the fat of the land and open up the windows of heaven and pour out blessings that I won't have room to receive!

That's why we sing, *Praise God from whom all blessings flow! Praise him all creatures here below! Praise him above thee heavenly host! Praise God the Father! Praise God the Son and*

*Praise God, the Holy Ghost!" (And) the command from heaven
is still, "Let everything that has breath, praise ye the Lord!*

That's why we sing, *All hail the power of Jesus name! Let
all the angels prostrate fall! Bring forth the royal diadem and
crown Him Lord of all! Bring forth the royal diadem and crown
him Lord of all!* (And) the command from heaven is still, *Let
everything that has breath, praise ye the Lord!*

That's why we sing, *"Holy! Holy! Holy! Lord God
Almighty! All Thy works shall praise Thy name in earth and
sky and sea.* That's why we sing, *Only Thou art holy! There is
none beside thee! God in three persons, He is the blessed Trinity!*
(And) the command from heaven is still, *Let everything that
has breath, praise ye the Lord!*

But, the second part reveals to us that sometimes,
obeying the command of God to praise God is like being
in a battle and fighting with a double-edged sword!
Sometimes when the pressures and the burdens of life
weigh us down, it can be hard to praise Him! Sometimes,
while praise is in our mouths, while hallelujah is on our
lips, while thank you Jesus is in our hearts we have got
to have a sword in our hands! Why? Because that same
devil is still out to steal and to kill and to destroy! Destroy
what? Well the accuser of the brethren is out to: Destroy
your praise! Mutilate your testimony! Kill your joy for the
things of God! Steal your worship! Make you abandon
your post! Have all of your good spoken of in an evil and

ungodly way! Cripple your dance! Dismember the unity of your spirit with your mind and your mind with your soul. Damage your reputation beyond repair! Wreak havoc and create mayhem in your life!

That's why when life is going good, we can't forget to praise Him! That's why in every season, we must remember that while we have so much to thank the Lord for, we cannot forget that it did not come without struggle! For many of us, the praise that we give was won out of a hard-fought battle for our lives! In every season, we must remember that our battle is a spiritual battle, which we must fight by spiritual means. For we wrestle not against flesh and blood, but against wickedness and principalities in high places.

In this spiritual battle, we can fight with God's strength, in God's way, and at the same time, give a worthy God worthy praise! We can declare to the world that no matter what it looks like our story is not over! We can say to the devil, "Devil, you thought that you had won, but because I learned how to praise him, this is simply a short, ugly, unhappy chapter in the book that is my life and I've got new mercies waiting for me on the other side of this mess!"

Sometime, we can look at some people and tell that they have not had an easy life. We can look at some people and tell that they have been through something! We can look at some people and tell that they are survivors! But there are those of us who understand what a marvelous thing it is to be forgiven by God! There are those of us who understand what a wonderful thing it is to be kept by God! There are those us who understand how magnificent it is to have the confidence that God will give us a second chance! How awesome is that miracle called a second chance! God will give you a second chance!

Sometimes you see folk praising the Lord as if they have lost their minds, while some of us sit back and say, "It doesn't take all of that!" Sometimes it does take all of that, and some more of that. As the hymn writer states, *You don't know like I know what He's done for me! He picked me up and turned me around; placed my feet on a foundation that will not fail! That's what he's done for me!* When you see folk shouting, crying, running, spinning, and jumping, leaping and knocking over chairs, that's the part of their testimony that they can't tell anybody but God!

Now if the Lord has done anything for you, you ought to go ahead and praise Him! Let everything that has breath praise the Lord!

# CHAPTER 11

# Better Than Blessed!

*And seeing the multitudes, he went up into a mountain: and when he was set, his disciples came unto him: And he opened his mouth, and taught them, saying, Blessed are the poor in spirit: for theirs is the kingdom of heaven. Blessed are they that mourn: for they shall be comforted. Blessed are the meek: for they shall inherit the earth. Blessed are they which do hunger and thirst after righteousness: for they shall be filled. Blessed are the merciful: for they shall obtain mercy. Blessed are the pure in heart: for they shall see God. Blessed are the peacemakers: for they shall be called the children of God. Blessed are they which are persecuted for righteousness' sake: for theirs is the kingdom of heaven. Blessed are ye, when men shall revile you, and persecute you, and shall say all manner of evil against you falsely, for my sake. Rejoice, and be exceeding glad: for great is your reward in heaven: for so*

*persecuted they the prophets which were before you. Ye are the salt of the earth: but if the salt have lost his savior, wherewith shall it be salted? it is thenceforth good for nothing, but to be cast out, and to be trodden under foot of men. Ye are the light of the world. A city that is set on an hill cannot be hid. Neither do men light a candle, and put it under a bushel, but on a candlestick; and it giveth light unto all that are in the house. Let your light so shine before men, that they may see your good works, and glorify your Father which is in heaven.* —Matthew 5: 1-16

$\mathcal{W}$ith the exception of verses 1 and 2, Chapter 5 of the Book of Matthew is a sermon. I believe that it just might be the longest and one of the most complete discourses of our Savior as recorded in the Holy Bible. It is a sermon that extends through Chapter 6 and Chapter 7, excluding verses 28 and 29. These verses read, *And it came to pass, when Jesus had ended these sayings, the people were astonished at his doctrine: For he taught them as one having authority, and not as the scribes.* It is practical doctrine in that Jesus gives us no visions of grandeur, but he gives us a model whereby we must live our lives as humans, as Christians and as children of the Living God.

How then does Jesus propose that we live our lives? Well, he proposes that we live our lives in a state of "blessedness." No matter what is going on in our lives, we must believe and know that we are blessed. It is a blessedness that has nothing to do with owning a house or a car, a boat or a plane. It has nothing to do with human accomplishments, accolades or honors. It actually has nothing to do with how we feel, who likes us, who accepts us, who supports us or who does not support us. Jesus began his ministry teaching us that we are blessed. In this passage of scripture, this sermon delivered on a mountainside, Jesus gives us eight beatitudes, eight blessings, eight benedictions, eight directives, or eight characteristics of blessed people. If we are going to be blessed, if we are going to be called Disciples of Christ, we must urgently answer the call of Jesus that beckons us to a higher righteousness.

It is that higher righteousness that brings us to the point of knowing that no matter what life brings, we will rejoice and be glad in the God who is our Creator and Sustainer. Quite simply, Jesus is calling us to live differently. Jesus wasn't preaching something about which he had no experience. Jesus was preaching about the life he had already lived and would continue to live until the day he hung his head and died. These Beatitudes, these blessings had to be the initial sermon of Jesus.

Ken Blanchard, co-author of *The Minute Manager* writes that in 1926, Dr. James Allen Francis penned a book entitled *The Real Jesus*. In that book, Dr. Francis included an essay he had written entitled "One Solitary Life." I have heard portions of this essay quoted many times, but never knew the origin. With interpretive descriptors of my own and for the purposes of hermeneutic and homiletic elaboration, I collaborate in the Spirit of God with Dr. Francis to describe our Lord like this: Jesus was born in an obscure village, the child of a peasant woman. He was poor, but he was born blessed! Jesus grew up in another village where he worked in a carpenter's shop until he was thirty—a skilled, but common laborer, yet he was blessed! For three years, he was an itinerant preacher. He understood what it meant to live in relative obscurity and that the preacher is led by the spirit and not by the dollar. He never wrote a book—no best seller. He never held an office—did not have to campaign for his place in the kingdom. He never had a family—although all who believe are his sons and his daughters, his brothers and his sisters, sharing the same Heavenly Father. He never owned a home. He understood birds have nests and bees have hives but the Son of man had no place to lay his head. He never went to college—no degree, but still blessed! He never visited a big city and never traveled more than 200 miles from the place he was born. The world was his passport.

He did none of those things one usually associates with greatness. Jesus lived a relatively obscure existence, yet He was blessed! He had no credentials but himself — humble, but blessed. He was only thirty-three when the tide of public opinion turned against him — betrayed, yet blessed. His friends ran away-no support system except that the Spirit of the Living God would hold him up, which made him better than blessed. He was turned over to his enemies and went through the mockery of a trial — persecuted, but still blessed. He was nailed to a cross between two thieves-humiliated and blessed. While He was dying, his executioners gambled for his clothing, the only property he had on earth — disrespected, yet blessed. When he was dead, he was laid in a borrowed grave through the pity of a friend.

Dr. Frances concludes this powerful essay by writing and proclaiming across decades that twenty centuries have come and gone, and today Jesus is the central figure of the human race and leader of humankind. The thesis of the essay is this: all the armies that marched, all the navies that have ever sailed, all of the parliaments that have ever sat and all the kings who have ever reigned put together have not affected the life of mankind on this earth as much as that one solitary life.

Jesus lived his life that had been blessed by God! Not just a solitary life, but also a blessed life! A called out life!

A purpose-driven life! Jesus knew what it meant to usher in a new world order. He knew what it meant to live a life devoid of comfort; Jesus preached these beatitudes because he had lived the beatitudes. He did not preach in a plush pulpit, but he preached on a common mountain. He didn't have any place to lay his head, but he received the kindness of strangers. I wonder how many of us can declare to the world that no matter what we do have or no matter what we don't have, we are blessed; we are better than blessed because our God reigns forever and ever and ever!

This discourse marks the beginning of the ministry of Jesus Christ. Jesus now began preaching and teaching right after he had been baptized by John the Baptist, and immediately after coming up out of His season of fasting and temptation. After a season in the wilderness, after being in a dry place, a deserted place, a barren place, right after He called just a few hardworking fishermen to be his disciples (Simon Peter, Andrew, James and John), Jesus was ready to begin His ministry.

It was now that Jesus saw his ministry drawing big crowds, and so He climbed up on a hillside while the crowds began to swell. People began to follow Jesus in great numbers because they had heard others talk about a man who was preaching and teaching and healing people. Jesus, right after he stole way from the crowds, went up on a mountainside to reflect and to ponder his ministry, his call, his mission. Jesus sat down and gathered His called ones around Him. He sat with those chosen ones who were committed to his ministry. He sat with those apostolic ones who had decided to drop everything and follow him. He brought close to him the ones who had taken on the mantle of the holy apprenticeship of the Gospel. He called them disciples. That's what a disciple is; not just a follower but also a committed, sold-out, blood washed, blood-bought follower of he who is the Lamb of God (a hearer and a doer of the Word of God).

And when he had come to a quiet place, a peaceful place, he sat down and began to teach his disciples. He taught them so that they might teach others. If you will allow me to use a bit of holy imagination, let me see if I cannot transform this passage into an anointed moment of verbal imagery so that we might gain a greater understanding of what it truly means to be blessed. I can imagine Jesus talking to his disciples and telling them that though life may be difficult, though there would be some difficult days ahead, I need to teach you how to first of all encourage yourself, before I send you out to encourage those who are in the crowds. In other words, let me teach you before you teach them. I'm teaching you so that when the crowds come, you will be ready to tell them what thus saith your God.

I'm teaching you now so that when they come to you with their issues, their problems, their disappointments, their faults and their failures, when the crowds come to you because the world has turned its back on them, let me teach you how to encourage, how to exhort, how to pray for, how to help them get free and stay free. I want you to teach them how to know that they are delivered, even when they don't feel delivered! Teach them how to rejoice even when they don't feel like rejoicing!

I can imagine Jesus looking down the hillside, and showing his disciples and asking them, "Do you see the great numbers who have begun to follow Me? Every single one of them has a need. Every single one of them has a story to tell. Let Me tell you who is down there in the crowd. In that crowd are people whose hearts need encouraging. If you follow Me, you will come across a few people who are not feeling very good about life. There are people who have situations and circumstances that they did not ask for, but somehow found themselves in, predicaments that are causing them sleepless nights and restless days.

"In the crowd, you will come across a few people who have had their hearts broken. You will come across a few people who will find it difficult to meet the challenges and the trials of life. You will come across a few people who have lost loved ones and who will lose loved ones. If you are to be My disciples, you have got to know how to strengthen and to encourage the people. Strengthen them and bring them to a point of holy resolve that no matter what happens in this life, amidst good report and evil report, TEACH THEM THAT THEY ARE BLESSED!"

I can hear Jesus saying, "Listen, they will come to you and you must do this: Teach those who are poor in spirit, that they are blessed, and that they will inherit the kingdom of heaven. My Father and your Father is rich in houses and land. Tell them that the cattle upon a thousand hills belong to the Lord. Teach those who are meek and humble; those who are content with what they have; be it a little bit or be it a lot, let them know that they will inherit the earth. Teach those who hunger and thirst for righteousness; I'm talking about those who have a great appetite for God and the things of God; let them know that they are blessed and that they will be filled with the goodness of the Lord simply because I am the Living Water and the Bread of Life who has come among them and sustains them."

There will be those who come to you because they are in need of mercy. Teach them to show mercy to others. Let them know that mercy suits every case. Remind them that they are blessed and that because they showed mercy, they shall receive mercy. And if you take care of God's people, God will take care of you. If you take care of God's business, God will take care of yours. Remember that it is written, that you have a mandate *to seek ye first the Kingdom of heaven and all these other needful things will be added unto you.*

There are those who will come to you whose hearts are right before God. Teach those who are ever striving for a pure heart that they are blessed and that they shall see God. Their heart's cry is give me a clean heart so I may serve thee. Lord, fix my heart so that I may be used by thee for I am not worthy of all these blessings. But give me a clean heart and I will follow you. Why? Because when their hearts and their minds are at one with their spirit, and their spirits are at one with their souls, they are the ones who can say whatever my lot, Lord you have taught me to say, it is well, it is well with my soul!

There will be those who come to you in the name of peace. We call them peacemakers. Not peacekeepers. Not those who will simple go along just to get along. But those who know that sometimes in life amid good report and evil report, we are required and we are called to bring peace out of confusion. Teach those who are peacemakers that they are blessed and that they will be called the children of God. They are blessed because they understand the Word of the Lord, which says, *The kingdom of God suffers violence and the violent take it by force.* They are blessed because they understand the Word of the Lord, which reminds us, *O how good and how pleasant it is for brethren to dwell together in Christian love: one Lord, one Faith and One baptism.*

There will be those who come to you when their testimony and their witness for God get them in trouble. Teach those who are persecuted for righteousness sake that they are still blessed and for everything that they have gone through for my sake that theirs is the kingdom of heaven. Some will be broken; some will be ignored; some will be persecuted; some will be ostracized, and some will be lied on, cut back, cut out, looked over, put down, set aside, and sawed asunder. But thanks be unto God they are better than blessed because that same persecution will drive them even further into the Kingdom of God.

Tell them not to fret, not to worry, and not to be anxious when people revile them, persecute them, and utter all kinds of evil against them falsely on my account. Tell them that they will be lied on! Let them know that they will be discredited! But also let them know that they are blessed, and if they would just hold on, hang in there, don't panic, don't fight, don't give out and for God's sake don't give up! Because great is their reward in heaven.

Some of us have got this thing called being blessed all wrong. We say that we are blessed if we have this or we are blessed if we have that, or we are blessed if we have accomplished thus and such, but let me follow in the footsteps of my Jesus and invert that which has been perverted and tell you that being blessed has nothing to do with what you have, but being blessed has everything to do with who we are. Being blessed is not an achievement, being blessed is an anointing. But on this day, here once again, Jesus speaks to those of us in this crowd who might not feel so blessed. Some of us don't feel like rejoicing or don't feel particularly blessed right now!

How can I feel blessed on this day? Well we can feel blessed in that Jesus at the moment of this inaugural discourse of his ministry ushered in a new order, a new way of thinking, a new mindset, a new way to look at life through all of its ups and downs. How do we know that we are blessed? Well, we find comfort in knowing that our God is a God of the cross and that He understands our grief. He understands our suffering. He understands our loss. Whatever we are feeling, God understands. And because He understands, we can find grace in the midst of grief, purpose in the process of pain and hope in the hub of heartache and mercy in our moments of misery.

Let these things assure you that you are blessed. Let these things bring you strength! Let these things be a consolation to you as you grieve! You are blessed! What I like about Jesus is that He will take your grief, take your mourning, and turn it all around at the end and says,

You rejoice! You be happy! You be glad! In fact, you be exceeding glad! More than glad!

God has allowed me to re-enter His house and this preaching moment to remind everybody that we are not just blessed, but that we are quite simply better than blessed! God has allowed me, once again, to approach this sacred desk, this holy platform and tell somebody who might not believe it, who might not feel it that not only are you blessed, but also that you are better than blessed! And so the relevant question of the morning is this, "What does it really mean to be blessed?" I hear folk say, "I'm blessed!" This state of being blessed, what does it all mean?

First of all, to be blessed means that you have the favor of the Lord upon your life. Favor means that you have his love; you have his joy and you have his peace. Favor says I don't deserve it, but I'm still blessed! Favor says that if it had not been for the Lord on my side I would have been swallowed up!

Favor says that the king's heart is in the hands of the Lord and just like the water he turns it whatsoever way he will. What is Favor? Favor to me is having God's undeserving, unmerited blessings surround you. Favor is the mercy of God. Favor is from God. Favor is being at the right place at the right time. Favor is getting a front row parking spot in a crowded parking lot. Favor is being the last one in a long checkout line at a department store and a cashier taps you on the shoulder and says, "I can take you right over here." Favor is when people just seem to want to help you. Favor is being a victor not a victim. Favor is the grace of God. Favor is the gift of eternal life. Favor is the forgiveness of our sins. Favor is Jesus dying on the cross for our sins. Favor is the fact that we are strong and well able to fulfill our God-given destiny. Favor is God giving you everything in this life He can give you without harming you. Favor is being a friend of God. Favor is having true peace and happiness that can in no way be obtained by anything in this world. James 1:17 says, *Every good and perfect gift is from above, coming down from the Father of the heavenly lights, who does not change like shifting shadows.*

Next, to be blessed means that no matter what the circumstances or the situation, God will take care of you. We have his power; we have his protection, and we have his constant provision. How do we know that we are blessed? Well, we find comfort in knowing that our God is a God of the cross and that HE understands our grief. He understands our suffering. He understands our loss. Whatever we are feeling, God understands and because He understands, we can find, grace in the midst of grief, purpose in the process of pain, hope in the hub of heartache and mercy in our moments of misery.

Finally, to be blessed means that we can be confident in the fact that we serve a God who will never leave us nor forsake us. We are blessed because He has given us His Holy Spirit, His Holy Anointing and His Holy Presence to guide us, to comfort us!

# CHAPTER 12

# Praise Him in Advance

*And as they were eating, Jesus took bread, and blessed it, and brake it, and gave it to the disciples, and said, Take, eat; this is my body. And he took the cup, and gave thanks, and gave it to them, saying, Drink ye all of it; For this is my blood of the new testament, which is shed for many for the remission of sins. But I say unto you, I will not drink henceforth of this fruit of the vine, until that day when I drink it new with you in my Father's kingdom.* —Matthew 26:26-29

There is something to be said about last things. Last words make us sit up and pay attention. Last words have more meaning, more significance. Some of us think of the last time we spoke to our mother, our best friend, or deceased father. Last words mean something.

Whenever a speaker is getting ready to wrap up, the clue words to let us know that the speaker has completed his or her speech is "in conclusion," or "as I bring this message to a close," or as Paul would say, *Finally my brothers, whatever is just, whatever is noble, whatever is pure, whatever is of good report, (you) think on these things.* No matter what words are used, we know that if they are the last, we are coming to the end of something.

Yes, my brothers and my sisters, last words mean something. We have come to learn that when someone dies the media, doctors, gossip mongers, rumor mills, family members, friends, curiosity seekers, fans and others want to know what the individual was doing in the in the last hours of his her life. (And)….in efforts to find out what might have caused an individual's death, we begin the investigation looking for any information, any clue, any hint as to what might have been the probable cause of the individual's death. And we all wait with baited breath to hear what the conclusion of the matter on the last hours of the life of the deceased. It all boils down to black dots on white paper we call a death certificate. It all boils down to a single word or short phrase that is the conclusion of the matter; especially if there is suspected foul play. Cause of death: Accidental drowning in the case of Whitney

Houston. Cause of death: Homicide by lethal injection in the case of Michael Jackson. Cause of death: Overdose in the case of Amy Winehouse. Cause of Death: Suicide as in the case of Phyllis Hyman. Cause of Death: Multiple gunshot wounds as in the case of Tupac Shakur. Cause of Death: Assassination as in the case of Martin Luther King, Jr.

However, in the case of Jesus Christ, it would be easy to say cause of death: crucifixion. However, we know that there are two sides to every story, and in the case of Christ, I would have two certificates. I would have one that denotes the physical cause of death and then I would have another denoting the spiritual reasons surrounding his death. I would sequentially list the conditions if any, leading to the cause of death and enter any underlying causes such as disease or injury that initiated the events leading to the cause of death. In other words, I would get to the bottom of the situation. The physical certificate would read something like this: Cause of Death, Crucifixion brought on by severe stress, even before the abuse began.

Medical writers have suggested several possible underlying factors contributing to Jesus' death including a fatal pulmonary embolism, cardiac rupture, suspension trauma, asphyxiation, a fatal stab wound, and the effects of shock. Shock, with complications of impaired blood clotting, is herein suggested as a medically logical mechanism of Jesus' death that well correlates with the biblical descriptions of Jesus' crucifixion.

That's one report; however, I am sure you know that there is always more than one side to any story. Therefore, here is another report; a report that reads like this: cause of death: redemption and salvation of humankind. The underlying causes were to take away the sins of the world and to pay the penalty for your sins and mine.

God decreed and declared it. The prophets foretold it. Humanity needed it. The world would have been damned to hell without it. God made him who knew no sin be sin for us. I'd be on my way to a burning hell without it. He was the only one who could have done it. There is no forgiveness without it, no repentance without it and no hope for eternal life without it.

With the former in mind, we are implored and challenged to walk by faith and not by sight. Therefore, when I can't see my way through, I prefer to listen to a God who tells me that I am fearfully and wonderfully made. I prefer to listen to a God who tells me that I'm bone of Adam's bone and flesh of Adam's flesh. I prefer to listen to a God who tells me that *In these last and evil days that He will pour of His spirit upon all flesh, and that His sons and His daughters will prophecy.* I prefer to listen to a God who will tell me that *I am His handiwork and that I can do all things through Christ who strengthens me.* I prefer to watch God move for me as he did for Lazarus when He told Him to come forth. I prefer to watch God move for me just as He moved for Daniel in the lion's den, or move for me just as He moved for Joseph down in a pit dug by jealousy. It is my preference to feel the Spirit of the Living God who can melt us, mold us, and shape us into the vessels of honor we were all predestined and pre-ordained to be before the foundation of the world. It is my preference to feel the Spirit of the Living God change that enigmatic something on the inside and make it manifest on the outside.

I'm glad I serve a God who gives me an experiential wisdom and a sensory knowledge of who he is: I can hear Him, I can see Him, and I can touch the hem of His garment. The Bible invites us to even taste and see that the Lord is good! Why? Because I've got to know Him for myself!

Why is it important that we experience God on such a deep and all-consuming level? So that when times get tough as they often do, when we give the best of my service and it still isn't enough and we run into that unavoidable life circumstance called sacrifice, we want to be able to remember that the same God we heard in the good times is the same God who allowed us to get close enough to him to touch the hem of His garment. I must be confident, that the same God whose Spirit became a shield about me and the lifter of my head, is the same God who is right beside me when I've been obedient to His word and yet I must still sacrifice something that I don't necessarily want to give up.

It is here in the Gospel of Jesus Christ according to Matthew, we find that this passage of scripture is in the context of the Passion narrative. However, the immediate context finds Judas agrees to betray Jesus to the chief priests. It is the first day of the Feast of Unleavened Bread and the disciples are making preparations for Jesus to eat the Passover. It was at the table of a certain man where Jesus was reclining with the Twelve, that while they were eating, Jesus changed the atmosphere of fellowship and brotherly love to the somber mood and attitude that sounded much like a prelude to death or a requiem for a dying man with these words, "Truly I tell you, one of you will betray me." He then identified the individual, not by name, but with the mysterious air of messianic mysticism. The words of Jesus were so stinging and incriminating that while the others could not even imagine such a thing and certainly not from among them, that the betrayer could not help but identify himself by asking, "Surely, you don't mean me, Rabbi?" And Jesus answers, "You have said so." Now with the betrayer having identified himself, Jesus would go on to institute the Last Supper. It is not a ritual; it is not a tradition; it is not ceremonious; it is not habitual. It is, the Last Supper. It is God's way of reminding us what Christ would do for all of us. It is God's way of reminding us that Jesus had the audacity, the boldness, the courageousness, the fearlessness, the foresight to give those of us who dare to believe that one man in the face of extreme suffering and pain could praise his God and his Father, my God and My Father, your God and your Father in advance of what he had to go through.

You see it was the Last Supper before Christ would predict the betrayal of Peter and the triple cry of the rooster in advance. It was the Last Supper before he would pray in a garden to let the cup pass from him, but resign himself to a nevertheless testimony if what he had to go through was the will of God for his life. It was the Last Supper before he would be betrayed by the kiss of a friend and sold out for thirty pieces of filthy lucre followed by a self-imposed death by suicidal hanging in the field of blood where the vultures and the maggots would feed upon the carcass of the betrayer. It was the last Supper before the sheep would scatter because the shepherd had been arrested and the disciples would hide because the teacher had given himself over to the ignorance and the arrogance of religio-political power.

It was the Last Supper before the false witnesses would lie on him, the Sanhedrin would testify against him, and still utter not a word when the false charges of Pilate came against him. It was the Last Supper before he would be stripped, mocked, beaten, spat upon, slapped plucked mocked and flogged. It was the Last Supper before he would be given vinegar to drink and refuse the bitter gall to numb the pain. It was the Last Supper before he would die between two criminals; one who would ask to be remembered and that same one whom Jesus would, on that day, in advance, promise a place in paradise. It was the Last Supper before the soldiers would gamble for his clothes, his enemies would mock him and subject him to ridicule and scorn as he hung suspended between heaven and earth. It was the Last Supper before he would cry out to God and ask his Father why he had forsaken him, tell us that the mission was finished, and then commend and commit his Spirit into the hands of God.

How is it possible that in advance of all of that, Christ could take the bread, give thanks, break it and give it to his disciples and tell them to, "Take and eat; this is my body?" How is it possible, that before He would go through all of that and then some, Christ would lift the cup, give thanks, offer it to his disciples and tell them, *Drink from it, all of you. This is the new covenant in my blood which is poured out for you (like libation) for the forgiveness of sins?* How is it possible that in advance of the whip, the hammer, the nails and the tree Christ would announce that He would not drink from the vine from now until that day when I drink it new with you in God's kingdom? It's all about knowing God for yourself.

You see, when my sacrifice becomes bloody and the stench of my of the wounds become more than my nostrils can bear, I want to remember the sweet aroma of worship and how God honored the sacrifice of my praise. I didn't feel like praising Him but I couldn't help myself. It's how I got over the last time. It's how I got the victory the last time when the vision of why I'm making the sacrifice in the first place isn't clear anymore and all around me is confusion and chaos and everybody is telling me that it doesn't look good.

When they keep telling me that what I'm praying for will never happen, and I know God to be a faithful God, I need to envision my Father like the prophet Isaiah did when he said, *In the year that King Uzziah died, I saw the Lord and He was high and lifted up and His train filled the temple.* In Isaiah's life, in your life, in my life and in every life when change comes, when the shift is inevitable something has to move, something has to break, and something had to die so that another thing, a good thing, a holy thing can live. That's the power of sacrifice!

Because when the weight of my sacrifice becomes more than I can bear and I find myself bending under the pressure, buckling under the load and I don't think that I can make it, I had to remember that Jesus carried His cross up Golgotha's rugged hill; not for Himself, but for you and for me. I remind myself that any sacrifice I make as a mother, a friend, a Christian, a preacher, a saint, a daughter, an aunt, a cousin, a co-worker, a servant and a care-giver only pales in comparison and can never compare to the perfect sacrifice Jesus made for the salvation of mankind. That is the salvific power of a Perfect Sacrifice!

Therefore, whatever we do, we cannot forget to tell God thank you for the ways that He has made and the doors He has opened. But even more than that, there would be no open doors or ways made without the unconditional love that Christ poured out on Golgotha. Never forget to thank Him for the nails! Never forget to Thank Him for Calvary! Therefore, I can't forget to thank Him for the Way of Suffering! Thank Him for the crown of thorns! Thank Him for the lashes on His back! It was the cross that bought my deliverance.

My last words is that in advance of my suffering, in advance of my sorrow, in advance of my breakthrough, in advance of the way you have already made for me, in advance of the enemies who have already been defeated, I will give God praise! I will praise him in advance for his wonderful works. I will praise him in advance for my healing. I will praise him in advance for my deliverance. I will praise him in advance for my liberty.

EPILOGUE

# A Final Word

$\mathscr{I}$t is an enormous privilege to be a biblical expositor. To preach God's Word is to stand in the pulpit or behind a sacred desk with God's Word in our hands, His Spirit in our hearts and His people before our eyes. In prayerful partnership, pastor and parishioners wait expectantly for God's Word to be heard and a transfer of spiritual wisdom to occur yielding a response to the call of salvation obeyed.

Sunday after Sunday, we deliver a weekly dose of compressed dignity, which gives worth to the human soul and deems flight to be appropriate, so that some broken spirit with a contrite heart would dare to soar on the wings of the Word of God. The sermon is more than just three points and a conclusion. It is more than an antithesis, a thesis, a relevant question and the subsequent resolution, which eases the tension between the two. The sermon is more than the sum of its conclusionary hoop. It is more than mere words spoken in the oral tradition. The sermon is a call for a visible confrontation between whom we are perceived to be and who God has predestined us to become. This becoming, this coming out, is a public outward display of an inward manifestation to yield to an immediate commitment to accept Jesus Christ as Savior and Lord. We attempt, under the divine unction of the Holy Spirit, to bring people to the mountain of decision whereby we must all climb the twin peaks of action and obedience. That is to say that we must *confess with the mouth, "Jesus is Lord" and believe in the heart that God raised Jesus from the dead* (Romans 10:9).

We walk through, live in, and negotiate our existence (our probationary existence) through a temporary and fallen world. It is a world whereby the gauntlet of belittlement has been lowered before us in the forms of personal attacks, insults, character assassination, satanic accusations, warped media images, obscene profanity, grotesque wealth and abominable waste wrapped in a package of insane jealousy that is blatantly an insult to the Holy character of a perfect Triune God. This gauntlet is an all out attack and an assault that attempts to debase the truth about whom God is and who we really are in Him.

Yet, I know my Redeemer lives. I know, I am sure and I am confident that God and God alone brought me out. I wish for you that same confidence and the same assurance that He has begun a good work in you, and He will complete it. Your mandate, your obligation, your commitment is simply to respect and obey the sacrifice required for your own salvation. While you are waiting and while you are working know that God is able, and then intentionally without the malice of forethought simply…count it all joy!

# NOTES

# REFLECTIONS & PRAYERS